Criminal Justice
Recent Scholarship

Edited by
Marilyn McShane and Frank P. Williams III

A Series from LFB Scholarly

Delinquency and Animal Cruelty
Myths and Realities about Social Pathology

Suzanne R. Goodney Lea

LFB Scholarly Publishing LLC
New York 2007

Library of Congress Cataloging-in-Publication Data

Lea, Suzanne R. Goodney.
  Delinquency and animal cruelty : myths and realities about social
pathology / Suzanne R. Goodney Lea.
      p. cm. -- (Criminal justice : recent scholarship)
   Includes bibliographical references and index.
   ISBN 978-1-59332-197-0 (alk. paper)
   1. Juvenile delinquency--United States--Psychological aspects. 2.
Violence in children--United States. 3. Animal welfare--United States.
I. Title.
   HV9104.L343 2007
   364.360973--dc22

2007009789

ISBN 9781593321970

Printed on acid-free 250-year-life paper.

Manufactured in the United States of America.

For my Dad, who was my first sociology teacher,

*and for Marty Weinberg and David Heise,
who together made me a sociologist*

Table of Contents

Acknowledgements

I would like to thank Sharon Barnartt and John Christiansen for offering encouragement and mentorship with regard to pursuing scholarly endeavors at a teaching-oriented institution and balancing the two in a responsible, sane way. Margaret Vitullo and my Dean, Karen Kimmel, have done all they can to ensure that I have had the institutional support to get this and other research done in a heavily teaching-oriented environment. I am immensely grateful to both of them. Teresa Burke has been wonderful at offering moral support and practical guidance with this and other research endeavors. Barbara Stock offered specific feedback on this manuscript and has become a terrific colleague and co-author.

I would like to thank Marty Weinberg for teaching me to be a rigorous, careful scholar and for keeping the faith. For all that I ever accomplish, I will be grateful to him. Eliza Pavalko taught me how to apply complicated statistical procedures carefully and confidently. Phil Parnell modeled a reasoned, humane, historically-informed understanding of criminology. Rob Robinson, Tim Owens, Tom Gieryn, and Jack Levin offered me support and encouragement over many years. David Heise taught me to think critically and creatively. Eric Wright and Jason Jimerson taught me how to be the teacher-scholar I knew I wanted to be and helped guide me towards a job I love. Many years back, at the University of Michigan in Ann Arbor, Michigan, Raymond Grew, Michael Kennedy, and Howard Kimeldorf taught this working-class kid that I could live a life of the mind, as a scholar. They guided me through my first research efforts and in my pursuit of graduate school. The Lee Iacocca Scholar's Program gave me the financial support to pursue an undergraduate education at the University of Michigan; without that support, I would never have pursued a doctoral degree.

Finally, I would like to thank LFB Scholarly Publishing and, specifically, Leo Balk, for their confidence in, direction with, and support of this project.

Thus, while all mistakes are my own, this work—like any scholarly endeavor—has benefited from much support, guidance, and feedback.

Suzanne Goodney Lea, Ph.D.
Gallaudet University

CHAPTER 1

The Presumed "Link" Between Animal Cruelty and Violence to Humans

"...unnatural cruelty is planted in us; and what humanity abhors, custom reconciles and recommends to us, by laying it in the way of honor."

-John Locke, 1705

This study examines human cruelty toward animals, a phenomenon that is cited by both lay people and behavioral scientists alike to be a harbinger of human-directed violence. Many people assume that someone who could beat a puppy or kick a kitten must be remiss of empathy and thus capable of all sorts of violence. The inherent assumption is that a transgression against, in particular, those animals with which many humans of Western cultures strongly identify and even anthropomorphize, indicates an especially cold and unfeeling personality that is potentially capable of any sort of cruelty. If a man shoots his dog, social philosopher Immanuel Kant, for example, reasons, he's not doing anything wrong to the dog, but he *is* doing something wrong to his own moral character and to all of those humans whom this character may affect, "for he who is cruel to animals becomes hard also in his dealings with men" (Rachels 2003:190-91). Kant referenced the ban of doctors and butchers from serving as jurors due to the carnal nature of their work as partial support for his reasoning (for a more elaborate recounting of this reasoning and the sway it has held over Western culture, see Franklin [1999]). The inverse is rarely considered, however: the Nazis, who were arguably uniquely cruel toward other humans, exhibited vegetarianism and adoration of their animal companions (Franklin 1999). How could people so capable of kindness to animals evidence such cruelty toward their fellow humans. I contend in this study that acts of cruelty toward animals *empirically* show no special association with acts of human-directed violence.

Other researchers have begun clarifying how common the practice of animal abuse, particularly by young boys, actually is within American society. Surveys of college students consistently reveal that many collegiate men report having engaged in animal cruelty during the course of their lives (Felthous and Kellert 1987; Flynn 1999; Arluke et al. 1999). Can a behavior so seemingly commonplace adequately serve as a means of identifying budding sociopaths?

To date, individually-perpetrated[1] animal cruelty has seldom been considered outside the rubric of, mainly, two discourses: (a) biographical accounts of identified extreme killers, which retrospectively assert that early episodes of

---

[1] I mean to exclude here the consideration of behaviors effected within institutional settings, for instance research using animals, animal trainers/handlers, farmers/butchers, etc.

animal cruelty clearly signaled these individuals' eventual violence toward people (Flynn 1988; Ressler et al. 1986) and (b) specific incidents of animal cruelty that are regarded as so sadistic as to elicit media attention. A propensity to engage in animal cruelty has been cited as evidence both of an individual's (a) familial pathology/disorganization (Ascione 1993; Ascione et al. 1997; Ascione and Arkow 1999; Flynn 1999) and/or (b) social alienation and resultant tendency toward violent expression (Arluke and Lockwood 1997; Arluke et al. 1999; Ascione 1993; Felthous and Kellert 1987; Hare 1993; Norris 1988). Usually, the focus of research has been upon what violence against animals might tell us about its perpetrators. Arguably though, the same tendencies identified post hoc in the biography of a violent individual can often be found within the biographies of his or her peers. How might one distinguish "boys being boys" from budding sociopathy?

Framing the issue as one of individual children abusing animals engages a particular level of analysis, one that is monadic and situational. Any identification of the patterns that might underlie this behavior therefore remains elusive. We might thus profit by refocusing our social analyses from any one cruel or "at risk" child to a broader examination of socialization forces. Rather than attempting to seek out particular young people who might be dangerous, we could instead work toward identifying socialization trajectories that accommodate and encourage anti-social impulses.

Challenging the pervasive assumption that animal cruelty is both rare and a harbinger of sociopathy, I aspire to document here the prevalence of animal cruelty within many individuals' life course trajectories. If this behavior is more common than presumed, an assessment of the social, psychological, and developmental functions that this behavior might serve is warranted. Perhaps this behavior is not even experienced as violent by its perpetrators. In fact, it may be an expression of boredom, an effort at sensation-seeking for "kicks" or "thrills," reflecting a vein similar to that tapped by Katz's (1988) research findings. By examining this behavior as more a social phenomenon than a matter of individual deviance, the cultural bailiwick that allows individuals to enact such cruelty within a context of banality reveals itself, as Scully and Morolla (1984) found in their examination of rapists' accounts of their experiences and motivations. Once rapists' own explanations of their behaviors were examined, a picture of a society that over-sexualizes women, and arguably even supports their being raped, emerges. One wonders what forces within American society have ostensibly earmarked animal cruelty as a horrible act while simultaneously defining groups that aide and shelter animals as "humane" societies. What is the presumed gestalt within such a context?

How Did Animal Abuse Come to Be Viewed as a Warning Sign of Sociopathy?

In 1963, John M. MacDonald posited that aggression towards animals could be considered one part of a "triangle" of pre-sociopathic symptoms, along with enuresis and fire-setting. Though most researchers have set themselves to investigating etiological precedents to Anti-Social Personality Disorder within a much wider scope than MacDonald envisioned (Gluek and Gluek 1950; Hare 1993; Newman 1987; Robins 1966), some researchers still assert the reliability of the triangle, or at least the part thereof pertaining to aggression toward animals. Despite critiques and conflicting data, discussed below, the notion that animal abuse is a pre-sociopathic symptom has grabbed hold of the public imagination, gradually achieving near-mythical stature.

Three factors have contributed to this popularity. First, sensational stories have borne out the proposed connection. Historically, we have the case of Pierre Rivière, whose 1835 acts of parricide were uniquely well documented and later compiled by Foucault (1975). Contemporaries of Rivière pepper their character testimonies and legal summations with allusions to Rivière's regular torture of birds and frogs and other such animals as, seemingly, obvious evidence of his cruel and heartless nature. More recently, reports of teenage school shooters' prior cruelties toward animals inevitably emerge after such incidents make headlines. Friends of the shooters recount that the shooter used to do things to animals. For instance, Kipland ("Kip") Kinkel, who killed his parents one night and then opened fire on his classmates the next morning, killing two of those classmates, is reported by a peer to have run over snakes with his skateboard. What the peer does not report is that the he knows of this behavior only because he was doing it with Kip (Sullivan 1998). Similar examples of reported cruelty to animals can be found in the post-incident background narratives of Luke Woodham (Pearl, Mississippi) and Andrew Golden and Mitchell Johnson (Jonesboro, Arkansas). It is important to note that the construction of biographical narratives about a person who has perpetrated unspeakable violence will inevitably be impacted by selective observation. Observers desperately seek some explanation for what caused the person to enact such horror.

This leads us to the second factor: MacDonald's (1963) triangle provides concrete warning signs for unthinkable behavior. It reassures people to believe that there must be some prior symptom evidenced by a teenager who kills his parents and then shoots dozens of classmates, or by a serial killer who tortures and murders his victims. We do not want to think that just anyone is capable of such acts. Animal abuse seems a good candidate for a behavior so "evil" that it must discriminate between good and bad individuals, giving us a simplified means of identifying at-risk youth.

A third factor that has contributed to the popularity of the MacDonald triangle is that the line between research and advocacy has become blurred, which may have inflated the perceived strength of the evidentiary support for the link between animal and human cruelty. Individuals and organizations with strong animal welfare agendas are disseminating, and even compiling, research on this link. For example, consider an excerpt from an ad in the September 2005 issue of *Good Housekeeping*, placed by People for the Ethical Treatment of Animals (PETA):

> Often, boys will be boys. Pulling pigtails and shooting spitballs may be harmless pranks, but when kids hurt animals, they often grow up to be violent criminals. FBI experts know that serial killers and rapists often have a history of animal abuse. Teach your child that it's wrong to hurt animals. If you know a child who has abused animals, tell the parents or the police before the child's violence escalates.

Here PETA cites data without noting its significant limitations. FBI experts base their expertise on the offenders they encounter. They are not doing scientific research; they are solving crimes. Access to their records and processes is closed and thus cannot be peer-reviewed.

Developing a heuristic opinion based upon one's experience does not render one an expert on the etiology of violent offenders. Furthermore, even granting that "serial killers and rapists often have a history of animal abuse," this does not imply that "when kids hurt animals they often grow up to be violent criminals." It is errant reasoning to suppose that the fact that a large percentage of violent offenders abused animals entails that a large percentage of animal abusers will become violent offenders. Of course, PETA's mission is not to clarify the nuances of statistical data; it is to help animals. Appealing to the tendency of animal abusers to harm humans is more likely to further this agenda with the readership of *Good Housekeeping* than would some of PETA's more radically pro-animal rhetoric.

Notably, some of the key players in performing and compiling research on this subject are also public figures in organizations that advocate for animal welfare. Randall Lockwood, who served as Vice-President for Research and Educational Outreach with the Humane Society of the United States (HSUS) until 2005 (he joined the HSUS staff in 1984) and now serves as Senior Vice-President for Anti-Cruelty Initiatives and Training with the American Society for the Prevention of Cruelty to Animals (ASPCA), and colleague, Frank Ascione, who has also served in an advisory capacity for HSUS, edited the compilation, *Cruelty to Animals and Interpersonal Violence* (Lockwood and Ascione 1998). In the animal advocacy role, it is expedient to present the link between animal-directed violence and human-directed violence as well-established. Thus, from a CBS news story (Hughes 1998):

> Gaining a sense of power and control through the suffering of another living thing is a very dangerous lesson that children learn often with animals as their

first victim," said the Humane Society's Randall Lockwood, publisher of a study on the link between human and animal abuse.

Similarly, the HSUS sponsors efforts, such as the ongoing *First Strike* campaign, which use promotional materials, workshops, and even celebrity endorsements to assert the "clear" link between animal and human violence. From a 1998 letter addressed by Paul G. Irwin, president of the HSUS until 2004, to members of the American public: "First Strike is attempting to educate the public to understand that a crime against an animal is a crime against society, and a child who abuses a pet may have deep, serious problems that sooner or later could lead to human violence." He continues: "And when you return the survey [about animal cruelty], perhaps you can send a gift of $10 to the HSUS today to help us publicize the connection between animal cruelty and human violence."

It is one thing to *advocate* on the basis of there being a clear "link" between animal cruelty and future human-directed violence, but, as a social scientist, one must retain skepticism; this is the basis of all good science. Perhaps the researchers involved do indeed keep these roles separate, maintaining objectivity in research alongside their public roles as animal advocates. Still, the convergence of these roles in the same persons may make the empirical support for the putative "link" seem unambiguous. When those with academic credentials, such as Kenneth Shapiro, executive director of Psychologists for the Ethical Treatment of Animals, over-generalize, "Virtually every one of these kids who ends up shooting up the school yard has a history of animal abuse" (Martin 1999), it is not surprising that the popular press take this at face value: in an article discussing the shootings by two Arkansan boys of their schoolmates and teacher, *Newsweek* asserts that, "Psychologists say that one of the surest sign of an incipient sociopath is a child who likes to tease or torture animals" (Gegax et al. 1998).

Additionally, there is now evidence that violent offenders proceed in no direct path from "practicing" on animals and then moving to humans (Arluke et al. 1999). What is often not reported by the mainstream press and what has not been examined very closely by researchers is that, for every child who abuses an animal and then shoots up his school yard, there are probably thousands of children who have abused an animal but have not gone on to shoot up their schools. In the *Rolling Stone* article examining the public construction of the life of Kip Kinkel, who killed his parents and then shot up his school mates in May, 1998, author Randall Sullivan (1998, p. 81) makes the following observation:

> . . . in the *Portland Oregonian*, a classmate named Jesse Cannon was quoted as saying that Kip was a 'Jekyll and Hyde' who talked constantly about killing and plotted a shooting spree while riding the school bus. What none of the papers told its readers was that until last fall, Jesse Cannon had been not only Kip's closest friend but also his principal partner in building bombs and shoplifting at local stores. Aaron Keeney was a source as well, recalling assorted scary stories that Kip told. No articles, though, mentioned Aaron's own tales, like the one he is said to have told about putting his pet hamster out in the middle of the road and trying to run it over with Rollerbaldes, or how, when that failed, he shot the hamster in the head with his BB gun.

It reassures people to think that there must be warning signs evidenced by a child capable of killing his parents and then shooting dozens of classmates the next day, and animal abuse apparently seems a good candidate for a behavior so "evil" that it must discriminate between good and bad individuals. Though not remarked upon at all in previous versions of the Diagnostic and Statistical Manual of Mental Disorders (DSM), animal cruelty is now listed as one of the warning signs of Conduct Disorder in the DSM-IV (1994). Pressure to pathologize cruelty toward animals by children compelled its listing as one of seven behaviors indexed to diagnose Conduct Disorder within DSM-IV.

In 1974, Goldstein proclaimed that the "fact" that early cruelty to animals is indicative of psychopathology is "already agreed upon." As a result of such rhetoric, animal abuse has come to be widely identified with sociopathy. Still, social scientific research, thus far, has yielded little convincing evidence to justify populist cries of outrage that posit animal cruelty within an animal-cruelty-to-human-violence progression paradigm, commonly termed the "graduation hypothesis" (Felthous and Kellert 1987). To date, there exists no no convincing empirical evidence that cruelty towards animals begets human-directed anti-social behavioral outcomes, despite such campaigns as the Humane Society of the United States' "First Strike" effort. In fact, some experts will acknowledge that there exists no such "link" but persist in promoting this idea because it helps with fundraising for animal protectionist organizations (author's personal phone conversation).

Much of the work that provides the basis for this claim is anecdotal and not especially rigorous. Liebman (1989), for instance, argues that animal cruelty is characteristic to the life histories of serial killers based upon just four case histories. Tapia's (1971) study of children who are cruel to animals proposes a list of characteristics that are common to such children. The problem with this study is that it examines eighteen case histories of children who were referred for psychiatric care because they were cruel to animals and, typically, otherwise violent. This group of youngsters might represent a uniquely anti-social set of aggressive persons. Rigdon and Tapia (1977), in a follow-up to Tapia's (1971) study find, indeed, that many in this initial group of children are still consistently aggressive several years later. This narrow sampling of study participants, however, does not tell us how common such abuses toward animals might be in the broader population. Maybe the animal abuse done by these young people sounds especially bad because it is in framed within a contextualized pattern of abusive, aggressive behavior. Still, the specific acts of animal cruelty themselves might not be especially unusual.

The few statistical studies that have been attempted suffer from (a) small N's and big conclusions (Flynn 1988; Kellert and Felthous 1985; Norris 1988; Ressler et al. 1986) and (b) non-representative study groups (Flynn 1988; Liebman 1989; Ressler et al. 1986). Too often, researchers have gone only to violent offenders in search of personal histories of animal abuse. Flynn (1988), Norris (1988), and Ressler et al. (1986), for instance, like Liebman (1989), only examine a study population of serial and mass murderers, finding that many of these individuals' backgrounds include accounts of animal cruelty. Though Flynn (1988) and Ressler et al. (1986) may include larger numbers of serial killers in their studies than did Liebman (1989), neither includes a control group. Beyond the possibility that these types of offenders might over-report such abuses so as to look meaner or tougher, as Arluke and

Lockwood (1997) suggest, the fact that a serial murderer, might have abused animals during his or her formative years is not necessarily significant. The idea that he or she might have intentionally abused a helpless animal indeed sounds horrible, but if other children who did not grow up to be serial murderers also abused animals, then the import of animal abuse in the psychosocial development of a serial murderer becomes less clear. In effect, one could envision the possible relationships between animal abuse and anti-social behavioral tendencies via Table 1.1.

Most research has not attempted to explore the animal abuse histories of "normal" individuals (Arluke and Lockwood 1997), or the experiences of those anti-social or violent individuals who have not ever acted out violently upon animals. Notably, there are several such individuals. Some notorious killers have, in fact, expressed feeling more a sense of affinity with animals than with humans. Dennis Nilsen represents one such case. When he was finally arrested for a series of murders in London, his central concern was the fate of his dog, which was, in fact, euthanized by the authorities (Masters 1985). Adolf Hitler and many of his fellow Nazi comrades were avid animal lovers, even vegetarians (Franklin 1999). Jeffrey Dahmer, who is oft-cited as "having abused animals as a child," in fact appears to have done no such thing. He instead showed a strong affinity for animals, only once causing suffering to an animal. In that instance, he was in primary school and became frustrated when an adored teacher to whom he had presented a goldfish gave the gift to another boy in his class. When Dahmer discovered this "betrayal," he poured turpentine into the bowl, killing the fish (Dahmer 1994). Though some might dismiss this behavior because it was directed toward a "minor" animal, such use of an animal as a proxy for one's frustrations may represent a worrisome motivational context. Other than this incident, Dahmer's

Table 1.1: Conceptual Model Illustrating How Animal Cruelty Relates to Sociopathy.

	Kind to Animals	**Cruel to Animals**
"Normals"	Presumption that a "good" person could not intentionally hurt or torment an innocent animal.	UNEXPLORED
Sociopaths	UNEXPLORED	Small-N studies of incarcerated serial killers suggest that these individuals commonly abuse animals during childhood, or adolescence. Some experts infer that such abuse is "practice" for eventual killing of humans.

"torture" of animals involved no such thing. He did have a strange passion for dissection, but he would explicitly select animals that had been killed on the country road outside his home for such explorations so as not to cause any suffering. In fact, as a teen, when he witnessed another boy run over a puppy, as so many boys in that age range seem prone to do, Dahmer was outraged and immediately severed the friendship with the boy, after ensuring the puppy was not hurt (Masters 1993). Harris (1977), referring to his contemporary criminologists' lack of attention to the gender dimension of crime, terms such oversights "conceptual blind spots." In effect, researchers themselves can become so entrenched in their particular worldviews, or perspectives, that they simply cannot imagine asking certain kinds of questions. Arguably, this is what has happened in the exploration of animal cruelty.

The studies of animal cruelty, which have been larger and more representative, have veered from attempting to answer the original question: "Does animal abuse predict sociopathy (or future human-directed violence)?" to instead exploring how animal abuse might be associated specifically with such phenomena as patterns of domestic violence (Ascione et al. 1997; Flynn 1999; Raupp et al. 1997). The original, broader question as to whether or not animal cruelty predicts human-directed violence, then, has still not been adequately answered in an empirical fashion. Though most work on the topic of animal abuse has focused upon the histories of persons in correctional institutions, there do exist studies that have attempted to provide, either directly or indirectly, a broader assessment of the extent of animal cruelty within the general population. The most read and cited of these is Kellert and Felthous' work, summarized in their 1985 publication. More recently, see Arluke et al. (1999).

Kellert and Felthous' (1985) study uses close-ended interviews of both aggressive and non-aggressive incarcerated offenders as well as never-incarcerated individuals to clarify how experiences with animal abuse differ among these three groups. Commenting on this study, Ascione (1993) remarks: "Although this and related research have been acknowledged to contain some inconsistencies and to share some methodological shortcomings (Felthous and Kellert, 1987), a case for the prognostic value of childhood animal cruelty has been made." This conclusion hardly seems merited, however, since about 30% of both the aggressive offenders and the non-offenders in Kellert and Felthous' study (1985) reported never having engaged in an act of animal cruelty. Of those who did report such activity, the 25% of aggressive men who propagated "substantial cruelty" actually represented only twelve men, each of whom reported five or more incidents of abuse. Why five incidents were significantly different from, say, three or four incidents (the categorization denoted prior to the "five or more" designation) was never clarified but seems an important point, as 16% of the non-offenders reported 3-4 incidents of abuse.

Felthous and Kellert (in Lockwood and Ascione 1998) are clear in their goals/biases:

> (Meanwhile), clinicians, jurists, school teachers, parents, and others who work and play with children should be alert to the potentially ominous significance of this behavior in childhood and the advisability of concerned, helpful intervention. Also, on a preventative note, if aggression to animals can become generalized to involve humans, perhaps an ethic of compassion and respect for animals can also carry over to humans.

These would seem to be noble, well-intentioned goals, but social policy guidelines arguably extend only from valid and reliable research findings. The presumption, then, that "aggression to animals can be generalized to involve humans" has not yet been reliably established (Arluke and Lockwood 1997; Arluke et al. 1999). In fact, Arluke et al. (1999), in a substantive, empirical study correlating reports of animal cruelty to authorities with criminal records (or lack thereof) find that there is no clear, progressive "link" between animal cruelty and future human-directed violence. Among those who were cruel to animals, some individuals had criminal records that included human-directed violence, and some did not. In cases where there were reports of human-directed violence, acts of animal cruelty that might have been reported did not consistently predate the reports of human-directed violence. In effect, some individuals seemed simply to be very aggressive, alternating between animal targets and human targets but following no particular pattern in their abuses. Of course, this study is limited by the fact that only reported incidents of animal cruelty or human-directed violence more generally could be collected.

More recent studies of the animal cruelty "link" mimic the famous Kellert and Felthous (1985) study. Hensley and Tallichet (2005a, 2005b), Tallichet and Henseley (2005), and Singer and Hensley (2004) have written a series of articles discussion the relationship between animal cruelty and human-directed violence using, like Kellert and Felthous (1985), an incarcerated population of 261 adult males. They find a relationship between abusing animals and conviction of more violent felonies, however, there are many drawbacks to using an incarcerated population only. They compare violent offenders with more moderate offenders but do not include a measure of non-felons. They explore how these felons learn to be cruel (Hensley and Tallichet 2005b), motivations for animal cruelty (Hensley and Tallichet 2005a), rural and urban differences in the commission of animal cruelty (Tallichet and Hensley 2005), and even whether whether or not firesetting and animal cruelty can lead to serial murder (Singer and Hensley 2004). In that article, they contend that information on the childhood and adolescent backgrounds of serial murderers is "scant." In fact, there is such a fascination with these cases, that more is arguably known of these individuals' backgrounds than that of any other offenders. Whether or not this background information is valid is another matter entirely, but it is certainly available from, usually, a variety of sources (interviews with friends and families, police records, interviews with the felons themselves).

Arluke and Luke's (1997) review of the literature examining the presumed "link" between animal cruelty and human-directed aggression cautions that the evidence is not conclusive. Ascione's (1993) review of the literature regarding this "link" recounts a number of case studies but few empirical studies. Many of the empirical studies reviewed are inconclusive. For instance, with regard to the firesetting-enuresis-cruelty to animals "triad," Justice et al. (1974) find support for the theory while Hellman and Blackman (1966) and Wax and Haddox (1974) do not. Price and Dodge (1989) find that attributional bias tends to inform socially rejected boys' levels of aggression. In effect, such boys tend to misread interactional cues, attributing hostile intentions to other individuals even when such intentions are not present. Such an attributional bias could work in a very similar way with regard to imputing intentions of animal interaction partners. Kolko and Kazdin (1989), however, in exploring qualitative accounts of firesetting behavior among children, add that a simple presence-absence model is insufficient in its explanatory power. In effect, the intensity, duration, and breadth of particular antisocial behavior may matter more than their frequency (Kazdin 1990). More recent explorations using carefully matched and/or longitudinal studies find that home environments seem to strongly impact teenage and adult behavioral outcomes. According to Becker et al. (2004), which examines sets of mothers and kids over a ten year period starting in 1990, children who are exposed to marital violence, parental pet abuse, and parental drinking are more likely to engage in firesetting behavior as teens. Firesetting, correlates in their study with a threefold increased risk of juvenile court referrals and a 3.3 times greater risk of juveniles arrest for violent crime. Marital violence and paternal or maternal harshness in parenting correlates with teens' reports of animal cruelty which then predicts higher self-reports of violent crime (if not official court detection). Currie (2006) finds that exposure to domestic violence correlates with more reports of animal cruelty by children. This echoes Flynn's (1999) work.

Making generalized statements that animal abuse predicts human violence based upon faulty logic and exaggerated research could be dangerous should well-intentioned parents or doctors start labeling children sociopathic or potentially dangerous based upon incidents of animal abuse which may have relatively generic and non-pathological in their motivations motivations. Many men, for instance, report that, as boys, they would seek animal targets upon which to fire their BB guns after tiring of the proverbial cans, open up a mammal to see how it worked, and aim for an animal on the side of the road as they were driving along in their car with friends.[2] According, however, to an article in a magazine for nursing

---

[2] These are trends gleaned from anecdotal data reported within a preliminary animal abuse survey I fielded in 1997.

practitioners (Muscari 2003), which asks *"Should I assess animal cruelty as part of all routine child health visits?,"* doctors and nurses should assume that, while some cruelty in the very early years may merely be exploratory:

> Pathological animal abusers are usually, but not necessarily, older. These children may demonstrate symptoms of psychological disturbances of varying severity, and/or may have a history of physical abuse, sexual abuse, or exposure to domestic violence. Professional counseling is warranted. Delinquent animal abusers tend to be adolescents with other antisocial behaviors, sometimes drug-, gang-, or cult-related. Both clinical and judicial interventions may be required.

As Piper (2003) contends in her article questioning the validity of the animal cruelty/human-directed violence "link," the hyper-explanatory power this mythical link has gained garners it independent power and a moral panic status. This can be dangerous when it is applied in clinical settings as fact.

This study will use a clinical study population to explore several questions raised by the research done thus far to investigate the perceived connection between animal cruelty and human-directed violence. I will first clarify the frequency of animal cruelty within my study population, as well as how reported involvement in animal cruelty and other anti-social acts during childhood or adolescence compares for men and women. I will then examine how other childhood/adolescent anti-social behaviors correlate with animal cruelty. Finally, I will assess how effectively animal cruelty predicts future human-directed violence and posit alternative models which might better explain the rationale used by perpetrators to explain violence done to animals. The use of a clinical study population, particularly a population drawn using the sampling method described below to over-sample anti-social individuals, helps to ensure that the study population represents a reasonably diverse set of individuals, in terms of their background with regard to childhood/teenage and adult anti-social behavioral patterns. Such diversity in the sample will allow for better identification of variables that might differentiate between animal abusers and non-abusers. Several in-depth interviews with selected study participants will also help to clarify the motivational context which informs animal cruelty.

CHAPTER II

Constructing the "Link"

Any discussion of a pathological condition, or social problem, almost immediately engages the boundary wars of two or more disciplines (Abbott 1988). With regard to defining, understanding, and treating sociopathy, sociology has largely removed itself from considering this phenomenon. In the last forty years it is the psychologists and psychiatrists who have staked out the job of making sense of this phenomenon. The framework employed by both of those camps is medicalized, and thus individually-focused. Sociology, by reintroducing context and social-level forces to the study of sociopathy, might endeavor to reclaim this domain of inquiry, thereby continuing the work of Robins (1966) and others.

Psychology represents a normative-based field. Hence, its clinicians measure phenomena via inventories of questions that intend to distinguish individuals who meet a given set of criteria from others who do not. Those who possess a set of traits that are not broadly present within a given population are potentially tagged as having the disorder indicated by these criteria. My criticism of this approach is that much is lost in the details. Each question that comprises a psychological diagnosis incorporates a large amount of information, but this subtlety is not considered. The meaning inferred when administering these questions is assumed to be "clear" by both researcher and subject, but many social researchers realize, based upon vast amounts of survey and interview data, that such shared meanings are rarely accomplished. Race, class, gender, and many other dimensions of the human categorization of experience compromise this process because they funnel perceived meaning in unforeseen ways for various individuals or groups of individuals. And, of course, subtle changes to the phrasing of a given question can also have a considerable impact.

For instance, this particular research project incorporates questions from the Diagnostic Interview Schedule (DIS), an index of various elements of anti-social behavior constructed as an array of experience-based questions (see questions excerpted, listed in Appendix A). Consider the question that asks about animal abuse:

> *When you were a child or a teenager, were you ever mean or cruel to animals or did you intentionally hurt animals (mammals, not insects, etc.)?*

A follow-up version of this question, administered in face-to-face interviewing off another schedule of questions administered during the same study posited a similar question, although this time without a specific focus upon mammals:

> *Have you ever mean or cruel to an animal or have you intentionally hurt animals, outside of removing vermin?*

These are, in fact, very different questions. A few respondents did answer yes to the first question but no to the second. A careful reliability check of the battery of questions that have been derived by psychologists to index various disordered states (pathologies) would surely unearth many other such discrepancies.

Such an item-focused, normative-based approach to understanding a psycho-social phenomenon ignores context. When we ask an individual about these sorts of experiences, using tools like The Hare Psychopathy Checklist (1991) or the DIS, we assume that a shared cultural understanding will allow a subject to "get" what a question is asking. The question may seem simple and straightforward enough, but, as noted above, there can be subtleties in the most seemingly straightforward of questions. If a researcher presumes that a given set of experiences consistently plays out in a particular way and drafts close-ended questions based upon those presumptions, we are placing much trust within his or her conceptualization of that phenomenon.

Per the phenomenon of sociopathy, available question sets meant to measure incidents of anti-social behavior arguably incorporate biases of race/ethnicity, class, and gender, at the very least. Do our checklists and inventories capture adequately, for instance, the range of experiences in which female sociopaths engage? We know from various researchers (Chesney-Lind 1998, Messerschmidt 1997, Steffensmeier and Allan in Zaplin 1998) that female deviance plays out within different outlets and patterns than, generally, does deviance expressed by men. Similarly, it seems likely that lower- and working-class men and women might act very differently than do their middle- and upper-class counterparts (or, as illustrated in Chambliss' [1973] article on "saints" and "roughnecks," class often implies a different response by authority figures).

In assessing, then, the social patterns that characterize animal cruelty, one might consider several dimensions of sociological theory. Mainly, my interest here in this study is to consider some of the social functions animal cruelty might serve in American society. The psychological perspective, though it may address the functions a given pathology might serve for a particular individual, does not consider the social functions that a perceived pathology might serve. Sociologically, however, one might reason that animal cruelty, for instance, could serve several social functions: (1) it might plausibly offer a release valve for individuals' frustrations, a function even psychologists acknowledge, although not in such a way as to consider how such releases might be socially informed; (2) it might serve as an expression of behavior learned from adult and peer role models; (3) it might evidence an attempt by some to seek sensation or stave off boredom; or (4) it might provide a realm within which young people might exercise identity exploration efforts.

These next sections will explore the sociological literature as it relates to each of the four potential functions of animal cruelty, as listed above. I first discuss sensation seeking, since this would seem the most common motivation, perhaps because adolescence in American society is characterized by an ambiguity of status. In effect, while some young people of middle-school and high school age are extensively scheduled into planned sporting and leisure activities, other members of this age group are faced with quite a lot of free time and little in the way of real, demanding challenges, tasks, or roles, which can lead to delinquent involvement (Felson 1998). Next, I discuss frustration and aggression release, which is the most commonly-perceived explanation for why someone might intentionally harm an animal. Finally, I explore learning theory and then identity formation, distinguishing between personal and social identity and incorporating a discussion of gender roles and their impact upon identity formation and perception. These categorizations seem to offer the most sociologically viable theoretical explanations for this behavior.

Sensation-Seeking

Katz (1988) elucidates a motivation for much youthful delinquency, suggesting that a great deal of this behavior can be explained via a discourse of sensation seeking. This would seem a plausible explanation for interpreting acts of cruelty by children. Perhaps, such cruelty is less a harbinger of sociopathy than a sort of release-valve for boredom.

In his thesis, *The Seduction of Evil*, Katz (1988) argues that young people pursue shoplifting, for instance, as a means of obtaining "sneaky thrills." Teens and preteens who shoplift, he finds, do so not because they need the items they steal. In fact, most of these young shoplifters report that what they typically steal is nothing they need or want. They shoplift simply for the thrill it provides. It is, they suggest, as if the items "call out to them" (Katz 1988).

This framework echoes that of Fine's (1986) concept of "dirty play," which suggests that young people use play to explore some of the forbidden or taboo aspects of their society. For example, young children might secretly "play doctor," which they sense carries some adult meaning that they are not supposed to understand. Perceiving that such play might be chastised if discovered by adults, children tend to engage in such play amid an oath of secrecy, which adds to the "fun" or thrill they experience. Arluke (2002) connects the "dirty play" concept to the accounts of animal cruelty histories he collected from twenty five of his students. He observed that many of these accounts resonate with the idea that young people are obtaining some sort of thrill from their actions. Additionally, he notes that these young people never discuss these acts after their occurrence— even with their peers.

That animal cruelty may indeed function as a means of sensation-seeking for young people is also suggested by recent literature on lifestyles of teens in suburban settings (Duany et al. 2001). While such environments may feature much adult-organized activities, there exists little for teens to do on their own beyond going to the shopping mall or movie theatre and little transportation for younger teens beyond the erratic bus. Young people—particularly males—in such settings may reasonably be expected to innovate "fun" activities, perhaps by exploding something with a firecracker or shooting something with a gun. Moving targets, such as animals, seem to be more exciting targets than, for instance, stacked cans.

Frustration and Aggression

Another explanation for aggressive behavior is frustration, or strain. Block's work, characterized by the 1977 text examining violent crime in terms of social environment and interaction, extends the Chicago School's perspective on the stains of urban life for, especially, young African-American men. Arguing that much urban violence is the result of widely-available powerful guns and turf wars, Block paints the picture of "hot" violent crime. Such crime is not cold and calculating but instead perpetrated out of frustration and rage. Henry and Short (1954) in their exploration of the relationship between suicide and homicide find that homicide, or outward-directed aggression, is more likely to generate when there exists an external force toward which to attribute one's frustration. Hence, "home" stressors like a spouse, kids, and pets, while decreasing the odds of suicide also increase the odds of frustration-driven homicide. Henry and Short (1954) observe as well that, due to social convention, men are much more able to express violence, but Schur (1984) notes that women, when they do exhibit aggression, are quite likely to act out in the home environment, against a spouse or child.

Sometimes an animal will come to represent the frustrations encountered through interaction with others (Flynn 1999). For instance, if a young person were to have a chance of gaining a "best" friend or a potential lover and that would-be companion were commonly distracted by, or attentive to, a pet, the young person might become filled with animosity for that pet and possibly do harm to it (author's research/interviews; Felthous and Kellert 1987). According to Price and Dodge (1989), boys who are rejected by their peers and/or are socially maladjusted are more likely to infer hostile intentions with regard to others' ambiguous behavior, with "others" including peers or, arguably, animals (Ascione 1993). Such personified abuse is more likely to be of a repetitive rather than an incidental nature. Such an individual may "stalk" or repeatedly torment a particular animal, developing, perhaps, an extensive fantasy around the animal. An individual may report having engaged in several such incidents, but each will be emotionally elaborate in and of itself. This sort of abuse may also encompass a sexual dimension (which is often vague or indirect) because the individual may develop an emotionally intense relationship vis-à-vis the animal (Flynn 1988; Hickey 1991; Ressler et al. 1986).

Research linking domestic abuse with animal abuse suggests that animal cruelty can also sometimes be an outlet for a particular sort of aggression. Children in abusive homes are more likely to exhibit an early first occurrence of cruelty, either toward an animal, sibling, or peer (Zahn-Waxler et al. 1984). In a sense, the abused child might transfer, to the animal, sibling, or peer, his or her frustration with the abuse he or she has experienced or witnessed in his or her home life. The child might do this to release frustration, or because he or she is simply imitating behavior he or she has associated as being "proper punishment" from the adult abuser in the household, which bring me to my next theoretical frame: learning theory.

Learning Theory

Another theory that proves useful in understanding many types of violence is the idea that people learn deviant or social behavior in the same way they learn pro-social behavior, via interaction with and observation of others with whom they identify. These others might be adult role models or admired peers (Sutherland and Cressey 1974). Just as a person might learn to "do stick-up," i.e., street robbery, or become a thief (Sutherland 1937), one might also learn to be violent towards animals, and other humans as well.

Athens (1989), for instance, proposes a model to explain the creation of "dangerous, violent criminals." Based upon extensive interviews with violent felons, his model hinges upon the idea that young people are first victimized by an adult in such a way as to feel weak and disempowered. They may also see others they care about, for example a parent, sibling, or pet, victimized in similar ways. Such a child vows never to engage in such violence but then one day "snaps" and exhibits violence in a public setting, for instance on the playground during recess at school where there are many other children to observe. The child may be acknowledged for his or her successful exhibition and then gradually come to embrace violence as a reasonable tactic for solving problems. At first, the conditions for its use will be minimal, but they will gradually widen because the child has a readily available rubric of justifications for using such violence under a broader array of settings. In effect, then, the child will have learned to use violence in much the same way in as their abuser used it.

Flynn (1999) observes that, many times, animal abuse and domestic abuse tend to go together. That is, homes in which a spouse or child(-ren) is (are) abused might very possibly house (an) abused pet(s). Here, too, children in this setting may observe a parent beating the dog for urinating in the house and come to view such treatment as normal or appropriate.

The key with regard to learning theory is that the young person will not only learn a behavior but also a context or vocabulary by which to neutralize, rationalize, or justify that behavior. Many people, of course, do "bad," i.e., socially unacceptable things, but an actor will typically develop some means of accounting for the act in such a way as to deem the act acceptable, at least under a particular circumstance. Generally, the framework of excuses and explanations which compose the context is learned from others.

Just as we are instilled with norms of behavior that orient to our gender, many of us learn negative, abusive behaviors via violence inflicted upon us within our home environments. Sutherland's Differential Association Theory (Sutherland and Cressey 1974) contends that people learn deviant or violent behavior just as they learn any behavior—via interaction. Widom's (1992) discussions of cycles of violence, Athen's (1992) theory of the origins of dangerous, violent criminals, and Strauss' (1994) efforts to document the prevalence and impact of child mistreatment clarify the details by which this process occurs. Children are beaten and brutalized by a parent and they may watch the abuser beat their siblings and/or the other parent. They learn either to behave in a similar fashion once they can achieve influence over others—or, in some cases, they learn to be repulsed by such behavior and to empathize with the victimized.

Animals, arguably, can serve as a mediator toward either of these outcomes. Some literature (Ascione 1993; Flynn 1999; Raupp, Barlow, and Oliver 1997) finds that children who are beaten in their homes start inflicting similar abuse on household pets. In effect, the children may act out the punitive role of the adult other as they try to discipline the pet, thus illustrating a central dictum of social learning theory: observation and imitation.3 They may also learn to take on such roles by watching older siblings. Some times though, the child sees his or her beloved pet being hurt by their household's abuser in ways similar to those the child endures. That child may come to especially empathize with the animal, which he or she comes to view as an innocent victim that cannot understand or avoid the punishments (see Flynn's [1999] work on domestic violence and its link with animal cruelty).

These rationalizations largely echo those noted by Felthous and Kellert (1985), in their study of abusers' accounts of animal cruelty. In many cases, an appeal to the ignorance of youth is made. In others, science comes to the rescue: curiosity, experimentation, etc. In still others, the animal is blamed for having misbehaved. Or, the animal might effectively serve as a means for expressing the abuser's frustration with the animal's owner. In a few cases, the abuse continues into the adult years masked as "mercy killing". Many times, the professed motivation is simply one of having been bored and in search of some excitement.

Gender Roles, Identity Work, and Deviant Behavior

It seems clear that gender, as with most aspects of human behavior, represents an important explanatory variable that potentially underscores all of the factors discussed, above.

---

[3] Here, too, then, the rationalization processes employed by children who experience abuse at home and then discipline a household pet are likely acquired via interaction with the disciplinarian parent.

Much of the sociological literature discussing deviance and crime observes that men are more likely to engage in deviant—and particularly, violent—behavior and that women's involvement is limited by their social opportunity structure. Anderson's (1999) work, and other work examining other settings populated exclusively by young males (Becker 1963; Katz 1988), provides a summary of behavioral patterns that seem to characterize these situations: an inclination toward "showing off" or boasting and an effort to project a "don't mess with me" toughness. Since much animal cruelty seems to occur within all-male situations, the social dynamic of all-male settings is relevant, particularly as it relates to identity testing along the social dimension of gender role prescription. However, the idea that women do not engage in violent behavior is increasingly suspect (Pearson 1998). In fact, women very obviously engage in aggressive acts. Researchers, however, may not be asking the right questions about the relevant contexts and thus be failing to identify such behavior.

Chesney-Lind's (1997; 1998) work suggests that all of our society's ideas about crime have been patterned by our gender roles and stratification patterns. In fact, most incidents of animal abuse appear to take place within small, exclusively male groupings. However, it may well be that women engage in abuse as well, albeit under different parameters. Chesney-Lind (1997; 1998), extending Widom (1986) considerations of cycles of violence, suggests that traditional examinations of delinquency benefit significantly by the employment of a field-observation/listening approach.

Much of the research conducted under the guise of classic studies of delinquency focused nearly exclusively upon men (eg., Chambliss 1973; Glueck and Glueck 1950). Women were dismissed as not being particularly prone to deviance due to a tendency to internalize the norms/expectations of proper behavior. At best, it was theorized that women would become more deviant as they gained more liberation (termed the "liberation hypothesis" by Schur [1973]). Chesney-Lind (1997) argues that a woman's obedience may be more a function of much greater monitoring and surveillance than some abstract propensity for girls to obey. In short, girls were kept closer to home. Theoretically though, girls' deviance could have been adapted to the home environment. In the case of animal cruelty, perhaps girls are more likely to abuse or torment household pets.

Messerschmidt (1997) suggest that crime is, in effect, an expression of masculinity, a means by which those deprived of traditional means of social success might gain social clout and respect. Steffensmeier and Allan (in Zaplin 1998) go on to argue that, because crime is so stigmatized vis-à-vis women, those women who do act out criminally tend to actually be more deviant than their male counterparts. The very terms we use for criminal identities tend to have masculine connotations: thug, mugger, killer, etc. (see Affect Control Theory [Heise 1979; MacKinnon 1994] for a discussion of such identity-linguistic connotations). Thus, we may have difficulty conceptualizing or categorizing a deviant or violent woman, though they may be equally prone toward deviant or violent behavior.

American cultural patterns generally deny women the externalized expression of aggression (while condoning, if not sanctioning, it for men), and thus aggressive behavior is deemed masculine (Henry and Short 1954). Such normative expectations muddy our very conceptualization of aggression (Widom 1986). For instance: a woman living within a Victorian setting might be more inclined than one living in modern times to appropriate the role of a "black widow." A Victorian lady had little opportunity to earn a living on her own; she was dependent upon her male "caretakers." However, if she were to murder a wealthy husband or father, she would legally acquire his wealth and maintain the security of a widowed woman's social position. This was one of the few means by which a Victorian lady could gain independence. We, of course, have little means of knowing how often such a tactic was employed. But, perusal of the historical record of female criminals (Newton 1993) makes it clear that there were many more incidents of black widowhood and other lone-woman-perpetrated murder (usually of other victims who were the woman's kin) recorded in the U.S. prior to 1950 than after 1960.

Borrowing from Sykes and Matza (1957) and, more recently, Scully and Morolla (1984), I use the concept of accounts to understand what acts of animal cruelty mean to their abusers. Accounts provide a glimpse at the motivations for acts that might be deemed cruel. Often, in terms of aggressive outcomes, we are called to apply a matrix of empathy. Some presume that empathy emerges almost "naturally," and early— perhaps by age five (Zahn-Waxler et al. 1984). I suspect, though, that children are often, by reflex, cruel to a wriggling, live creature that is smaller than them, and that empathy is very much a learned trait. And, like anything that is learned, it is acquired via social interaction.

Part of my interest here is the extent to which non-human "others" can elicit in humans the same kinds of symbolic processes that underlie the "looking-glass self." It is arguably much easier to rationalize or neutralize the "feelings" of a non-human other since the "other" in such a case can offer no challenge to one's rationalizations. In fact, it seems likely that some individuals, perhaps the "badass" characterized above, for instance, might not feel at all compelled to rationalize harming an animal.

From the sociological vantage point, humans behave according to their impressions of how they perceive themselves to be seen by others. Using a process termed the "looking-glass self," humans gauge the impression others seem to have of them by attempting to interpret others' reactions to them (Cooley 1902). Based upon such reflections, individuals begin to think of themselves in terms of various identities (Stryker 1968). One may come to think of oneself as a good student, for instance, if one is praised by teachers and achieves good marks. Such identity-formation can also work in a negative direction, as well. For instance, if an individual is repeatedly characterized a "loser" by his or her peers, he or she will likely begin to feel that he or she is a "loser." Such an individual may begin acting out in ways that confirm this view of self, perhaps avoiding academic, athletic, or social achievement. What sociologists term the symbolic interactionist perspective suggests, then, that identity formation unfolds in much the same way as a marble bouncing about a pachinko game. As we collide with others' views and demands of us, we are funneled down particular pathways.

In effect, then, young people— particularly men who are much more able to explore a "tough" or "badass" social identity due to this culture's pervasive gender norms (Katz 1988) may attempt to appropriate this social identity so as to fit in with peers or alienate "boring" adults. Such a young person might, then, go along with peers on an expedition to shoot at neighborhood cats or attempt to run over animals in cars. However, once such violence is enacted, some young people may find that they empathize with the animal if it is injured or killed. In such a case, this young person may feel much guilt over what she or he did to the animal. This may discourage the young person from incorporating this "tough" role as a personal identity (see Owens and Goodney [2000] for a more elaborated discussion of the dynamics of guilt and identity formation). While a young person may have many social identities from which to appropriate, not all of these may feel to be a good match for his or her personal identity context (Rubington and Weinberg 2005).

As a young adult, a teenager will begin testing potential identities. Though some young people seem to commit to a "badass" identity fairly quickly, many young people are arguably just "test-driving" a social identity, in accord with Katz's (1988) argument that deviance, particularly that perpetrated by young people, is largely driven by an inclination toward sensation-seeking and looking "tough" or "cool." When young people do "bad" things, the reactions of their peers will confirm or disconfirm their sense of commitment to such a negative identity (Ulmer 2000). In most cases of reported animal abuse, the activity is reported to have occurred in the company of others.

If an individual were, for instance, deemed a "badass" by some of his or her peers, s/he would likely begin to act tough and mean in an effort to confirm this label.4 For

---

[4] See Lemert (1951) and Katz (1988), as well as Athen's (1992) discussion of how 'dangerous violent criminals' come to find positive social support, or feedback, for a mean or cruel demeanor.

such individuals as these, animal abuse may be just one of many acts of social deviance affected in an effort to project a "badass" persona. Thus, the animal abuse may, in and of itself, have no special significance to this individual. He or she may readily acknowledge engaging in such behavior and perhaps even boast to peers of his or her exploits, citing them as demonstrations of his or her capacity for cruelty. In fact, because this behavior may be perceived as instrumental and non-significant, some individuals who have perpetrated animal cruelty may completely forget about past incidents of cruelty until giving an interview on the topic.

I will return to the theoretical framework outlined above during my concluding discussion, below, in which I will attempt to model the motivational contexts that underlie animal abusers' accounts of abuse. First, however, I would like to briefly review here some of the literature exploring the intersection of animal cruelty and human-directed violence, as well as some relevant sociological theories of delinquent behavior, so as to orientate the quantitative dimension of this study.

My key objective with regard to the quantitative portion of this study is to better clarify the extent of animal cruelty within a community-based sample. Hirschi (1969) and, later, Schur (1973) suggest that most humans are inclined to engage in deviant, and even criminal, behavior. The fewer social controls there are upon one's behavior, the more likely one is to act in a deviant, or anti-social, manner. Such controls can be obligations, or threats of sanctions. Since not everyone can be socially controlled at all times, most everyone is tempted to engage in deviant behavior. For every deviant or criminal act that is detected by some authority, there are likely several similar acts that go undetected. I therefore suspect that animal cruelty is likely to be more common than most Americans assume, even if it may not be well-reported or detected. Depending on who is doing the cruelty and under what conditions and in what locale, an act of animal cruelty is more or less likely to be reported. For instance, if one leaves one's dog panting in a hot car, this is likely to be reported. If one throws one's dog down the stairs for misbehaving, this is not likely to be reported.

A Canadian study (Offord et al. 1991) found, using a census-based sample, that about 2% of 12-to-16-year-olds were said to be engaging in acts of animal cruelty, based upon mothers' reports. When children were asked directly about their cruelty toward animals, the self-reported rate of such acts was nearly 10%. Interpretations of "cruelty" as well as the secretive nature of most such abuse likely explains the difference in reported rates—and may even suggest that the 10% rate is also underreported. Some children, asked directly, may have misunderstood the question, been ashamed to say they had been abusive, or even have forgotten that they had engaged in such behavior.

Specifically with regard to animal cruelty enacted during childhood, Arluke's (2002) study of college students' retrospective accounts of animal cruelty give strong suggestion that children may experience animal cruelty as a sort of "dirty play," extending Fine's (1986) research on children's use of play to explore taboo subjects and power dynamics. Arluke (2002) suggests that children may participate in such "play" but then simply outgrow such behavior. The idea that engaging in animal cruelty during childhood might lead to human-directed violence later in life is rendered dubious by Arluke et al.'s (1999) finding that there is no linear path progressing from animal cruelty during childhood to human-directed violence in adulthood. More likely, extending Lemert's (1951) labeling theory, the more one is labeled as a violent or aggressive individual, the more likely one will be to engage in violent or aggressive acts as one ages. In effect one commits to a violent identity, an idea echoed in Athens' (1992) work examining the "creation of dangerous, violent criminals." Importantly, per Schur's (1973) theory of radical non-intervention, the very process by which authority figures exercise their authority upon children and teens who are acting in anti-social ways out arguably ensures that the labels used to identify the socially inappropriate behavior will likely become cemented into the formative identity process of the so-labeled young person. Schur's advice: "Leave kids alone wherever possible (1973:155)." Typically, if left alone, children will simply outgrow such behavior and, thereby, not commit to an anti-social identity pattern.

Specific to men, one might reasonably suspect that such patterns of labeling might apply more to them than women based upon Harris' (1977) work, which finds that men are more likely to be officially labeled as deviant. Additionally, drawing from Matza's (1964a) subterranean drift theory, masculine cultural norms are more likely to glamorize violent behavior. Hence, among men who are committed to a masculine identity, tendencies to boast about acts of cruelty or mischief tend to emerge. Engaging in such "bad" behavior, within this sort of a context, becomes, then, a show of strength, toughness, or courage.

The research presented below attempts to puzzle out the frequency, function, and meaning of acts of animal cruelty in this society. How common is such behavior? Is such behavior more common among men than among women? What other behavior is associated with animal cruelty during childhood/adolescence? Does animal cruelty correlate with adult violence? This study aspires to use sociology's empirical tradition to examine these questions. The next chapter outlines the methodological procedures employed to accomplish this task.

CHAPTER III

Methodological Procedures

This project examines several hypotheses that promise to better illuminate the characteristics of the claimed link between cruelty to animals and violence toward humans. This chapter outlines the design of this study, the characteristics of the sample used, the operationalization of the study's measures, and the protocol followed in collecting the interview data used in this study.

Study Design

This study aspires to address the dearth of information available that empirically examines the presumed connection between animal cruelty enacted during childhood or adolescence and violent behavior evidenced later in life. As discussed above, there exist a few studies that attempt to empirically address this question, but most of these examine only incarcerated populations (Kellert and Felthous 1985), convenience samples (Arluke 2002; Flynn 1999), or idiosyncratic accounts (Flynn 1988; Norris 1988). The data used in this study generated from a community sample collected by Dr. Peter Finn through the

Indiana University Clinical Psychology Department. Some of the questions used in this study included sections of the Diagnostic Interview Schedule (DIS) protocol (see Appendix A for the list of questions used). The DIS inventory incorporates scores of questions that ask respondents about anti-social behaviors in which they may have engaged. Some of the questions refer to events that may have occurred during childhood/adolescence. Other questions ask about the same acts but refer to their incidence during adulthood (after age 15).

For my interests, the availability of response data for 570 respondents relating to questions about animal cruelty and many other anti-social behaviors was intriguing, particularly since this data included questions relating to both childhood/teenage and adult years. This allows for some comparison of behavior patterns over time, as well as a chance to examine the correlation between animal cruelty and other anti-social behaviors during childhood/adolescence. I used logistic regression procedures to examine the extent to which animal cruelty during childhood/adolescence predicts adult violence.

I supplement the quantitative data with open-ended interview data collected from 21 of the initial 570 respondents. This qualitative data allowed a chance to explore how study participants remember, explain, and recount acts of animal cruelty that they may have witnessed or enacted as a child or young adult.

The Sample

This study uses a set of quantitative data that examines the behavioral patterns of 570 young people recruited from Bloomington, Indiana. The study participants who took part in this research were over-sampled for anti-social personality traits.

The Bloomington, Indiana, community, population 69,291, is characterized by a highly educated population. Of the population of residents age 25 and older, 91.2% have a high school degree and 54.8% have at least a four-year university degree. This would explain the mean educational level being 14.24 for this study population. Only 12.7% of residents of Bloomington are under age 18, while just 7.9% of the population is age 65 or older. Being a college town, Bloomington is populated by a fairly young population. This would explain the relatively young mean age of this study group, which is just about 21 years of age. The gender composite for the city indicates that 51.4% of the population is composed of women, which corresponds closely to the gender breakdown for this population. Approximately 87% of the Bloomington population is white. The largest minority groups are Asians (5.3%), Blacks (African-Americans) (4.0), and Hispanics and Latinos (2.5%). The race/ethnicity breakdown for this study population is 83.7% white and 16.3% non-white, which combines Asians, Blacks/African-Americans, Hispanic/Latinos, and members of other racial/ethnic groups. The specific breakdown of membership percentages for groups compiled into the non-white category closely approximates the representation of these groups within the broader Bloomington population.

Recruitment of Participants

Recruitment for this study was designed to attract an over-sampling of anti-social personality types of respondents. The initial study for which this data was collected investigates disinhibition and alcohol abuse. Widom's (1992) method of inducing responses from persons who have traits composing disinhibition, a characteristic associated with Antisocial Personality Disorder (ASP) as the trait of "impulsiveness" (DSM-IV 1994, employs advertisements in newspapers inviting participation in a research study. These ads are crafted to attract three types of persons using the following phrasings: (1) "adventurous, carefree individuals who have led exciting and impulsive lives" or "daring, rebellious, defiant individuals," (2) "persons interested in psychological research," and (3) "quiet, reflective, introspective persons." The first of these phrasings, Widom finds, reliably attract individuals with a strong propensity toward disinhibition. These ads were placed in papers throughout Bloomington, Indiana, so as to attract (1) highly disinhibited, (2) somewhat disinhibited, and (3) highly inhibited persons, respectively. Subjects who responded to these ads and who were selected to participate in the study were paid $7/hour for their time. This study, which concluded in Summer, 2000, was conducted by Finn et al. and entitled "Disinhibition and Risk for Alcohol Abuse" (Protocol #97-159 with the Indiana University-Bloomington's Human Subjects Committee).

I recruited interview subjects by selecting individuals from the initial subject pool who either identified as an animal abuser or as a non-abuser, in response to DIS Question #9. I interviewed both admitted abusers and declared non-abusers to assess whether there were any relevant differences between these groups. I also included male and female study participants, as well as some who were categorized as ASP and some who were not. Laboratory assistants phoned lists of qualified (preselected, based on DIS Question #9 and other criteria) study participants and invited them to take part in an interview about "their interactions with animals, both positive and negative." Participants were offered $10 to participate in a one-time interview lasting, usually 1-1.5 hours. A total of 21 interviews were collected.

The Data

My data includes 575 individuals (cases). Only five of these cases had to be dropped due to incomplete case information. Study participants were paid for their time and given routinized question protocols in person by trained interviewers, so the data collected is quite complete and generally consistent. For instance, if one triangulates response data for two similar questions, one generally finds that the responses to both items will be consistent. As part of the original study, the Diagnostic Interview Schedule (DIS) behavioral checklist was administered (See Appendix A). This survey incorporates questions which operationalize many of the DSM symtomological criteria for ASP and its precedent Conduct Disorder (CD).

Measures

This study incorporates two types of questions, as used within the Diagnostic Interview Schedule (DIS). The first type of questions asks subjects about behaviors during the child/teen years. These questions may use various euphemisms, i.e. "when you were a kid" or "when you were a child or teenager," but the intent is to capture behavior occurring before age fifteen, in accordance with the guidelines of the DSM-IV (1994), which categorizes "Conduct Disorder" as symptoms present before age fifteen. The second type of question asks about behaviors occurring since the age of 15. It is probable, of course, that some subjects included behavior occurring during the later teen years (15-19) as well when answering the questions about behavior occurring "prior to age 15." It is impossible to assume that someone answering a question like this as an adult would be able to specifically recall whether remembered events occurred at age 14, 15, or 16, for instance. For the purposes of this study, however, it is not so significant if "childhood" behaviors include acts done at age 14 or 17. Mainly, my interest is in examining acts occurring during the childhood and teen years, termed here as in terms of how the pattern of those involvements might predict adult anti-social behavior.

For the purposes of psychological inventories, the convention for identifying anti-social behavioral patterns is to examine whether there exists an enduring trajectory, i.e., did the person's behavior begin in childhood/adolescence and continue into adulthood. The use of the age of 15 as a cut-off for the corpus of "childhood/teenage behavior" allows, ideally, for any anti-social tendencies appearing in the late teenage years to carry less weight in the overall picture of formative behavioral patterns. Many young people will engage in some anti-social behavior during the teenage years and then quickly outgrow these tendencies as they reach young adulthood. Examining patterns split across the childhood/adolescence and adult periods thus allows one better to identify cases where there is a lifetime of anti-social behavior.

Animal Cruelty

Operationalizing the definition of animal cruelty presents a number of challenges:

- The type of animal could matter.

- The type of cruelty employed also seems an important consideration: teasing, inducing physical suffering, sexual touching, and killing have all been indexed as abusive (Flynn 1999; Felthous and Kellert 1987; Kellert and Felthous 1985).

- The setting matters: wanting to see the insides of an animal is considered culturally appropriate in biology class but rather sadistic if enacted upon a pet dog.

Flynn (1999) discerned among (a) subjects who had killed a stray or wild animal, usually with firearms, (b) those who had hurt or tortured an animal (shooting, stabbing, burning, blowing up, or poisoning the animal), and (c) those who had killed a pet. Notably, and this will become more relevant in later sections of this thesis, those respondents who had killed an animal were least likely to repeat such an act of cruelty. Contrarily, were the animal simply hurt, recidivism rates were quite high (45%). If one reported killing one's own pet, one seemed also quite likely to repeat such behaviors.

Ascione (1993), in his review article, offered a definition behavior that aimed itself toward the "intentional" causing of unnecessary pain, suffering, distress, or death, or behavior that was deemed "unacceptable." Kellert and Felthous (1985; also see

Felthous and Kellert 1987) and Flynn (1999) incorporate intentionality, or "knowingly" or "deliberately" inflicting pain or torture upon an animal, into their definitions. A failure to intervene or a delight in watching peers engage in cruelty may also be deemed troubling, or cruel in itself. These behaviors arguably fall within the definition of socially unacceptable behavior, but it is difficult to specify what defines such behavior within this context (or in most other settings). A rural family would not likely regard pulling the wings off fireflies in the summertime or shooting stray cats in the head as especially cruel, whereas an urban, upper-middle class individual quite likely would.

I operationalize animal cruelty using Question #9 of the Diagnostic Interview Schedule (DIS; see Appendix B): "When you were a child or a teenager, were you ever mean or cruel to animals or did you intentionally hurt animals (mammals, not insects, etc.)?" The responses are: "No", "Occasionally", and "Frequently." However, I convert this into a dichotomous "yes" or "no" variable by collapsing the "occasionally" and "frequently" response options into one category. Note that six measures #7, #8, #9 , #10, #11, and #19, were originally coded according to response options "0," "1," and "2," with 0 denoting that the respondent had never engaged in the specified act, "1" indicating that the respondent had occasionally engaged in the behavior, and "2" marking that the study participant had often participated in the specified behavior. Extremely few respondents—typically only 3-5 individuals most any particular DIS variable—chose "2" in response to any of the DIS questions, and so the response option categories were collapsed into a "0-1," or "no-yes" format.

The following table illustrates the gender breakdown for the animal cruelty measure.

Table 3.1. *Distribution of Study Participants by Gender and Admitted Abuse of Animals.*

	No	Occasionally/ Frequently	N
Men	220	63	283
Women	278	14	292

Since individuals in this study who self-identify as abusers are responding to a broad, general prompt that measures an array of cognitive interpretations (i.e. some would deem pulling the wings off a fly to be abusive, while others could rationalize drowning a kitten), the reliability of responses to this question may be somewhat questionable. Some people may answer negatively to this prompt when it is asked within a battery of questions but then "remember" incidents if they are specifically questioned about their involvement with and possible mistreatment of animals. Also, as there is no choice to indicate that one had engaged in a particular category only once, there is no way by which to adequately gauge the importance of frequency in these measures, and this could well be a significant dimension to consider by way of explaining violent adult behavioral outcomes.

Other Measures of Childhood/Teenage Anti-Social Behavior

Table 3.2 summarizes the descriptive statistics for the measures used in this study. Please see Appendix A for the exact wording of each measure used. Most of the DIS items were used to inventory childhood/adolescent behavior. Only DIS items #38 and #39 measure adult behavior; those items are used as outcome variables in the logistic regressions, as proxies for adult violence (see below). Several demographic measures are also included in Table 3.2.

Logistic Regression: Dependent Variables

There were three possible measures I could have used to operationalize adult violence. These included a measure of domestic violence and two measures of adult fighting behavior. The question about domestic violence is worded as "hitting or slapping" one's spouse or long-term partner, and the response rate to this question seemed somewhat misleading. More women than men answered in the affirmative, but this could have been an artifact of the wording, in particular "slapping," a behavior many men may not identify as doing. Lottes and Weinberg (1997), however, in their study comparing rates of reported sexual coercion among university students in the United States and Sweden, found that U.S. men reported higher rates of non-physical sexual coercion than did Swedish men. They posited that this was perhaps due to (a) higher general rates of violence in the U.S. or (b) an effort by American women to enact aggressive roles in sexual interactions that were traditionally occupied by men. Finally, because the average age of the respondents in this study was quite young, there is less chance that the study participants may have had occasion to marry or live with a romantic partner.

There were a few other measures available on the DIS that measured adult violence, such as robbery or rape, but the response rate to these questions was extremely small. The two most usable measures of adult violence, then, were fighting and fighting with weapons, which are the measures

I used here. These were operationalized as yes-no variables, and, for the logistic regressions, these variables were pooled so as to create a larger group of study participants who admitted some kind of violence.

Table 3.2. *Descriptive Statistics for the Measures Used in this Study (N = 570)*

Measure	Mean[5]	Standard Deviation	Range
DIS 2: In Trouble at School	.29	.45	0-1
DIS 4: Suspended	.26	.44	0-1
DIS 5: Expelled	.13	.38	0-1
DIS 7: Fighting	.19	.39	0-1
DIS 8: Fighting w/Weapons	.08	.27	0-1
DIS 9: Animal Cruelty	.14	.34	0-1
DIS 10: Bullying	.13	.34	0-1
DIS 11: Hurting Siblings	.20	.40	0-1
DIS 13: Lying	.38	.47	0-1
DIS 15: Stealing	.52	.50	0-1
DIS 17: Vandalism	.35	.48	0-1
DIS 18: Firesetting	.27	.45	0-1
DIS 19: Juvenile Arrest	.13	.38	0-1
DIS 38: Fighting as an Adult	.18	.38	0-1
DIS 39: Fighting w/Weapons as an Adult	.07	.25	0-1
Sex 0 = Female; 1 = Male	.49	.50	0-1
Age	20.95	1.99	18-26
Education	14.24	1.62	8-20
Ethnicity 0 = White; 1 = Non-White	.84	.37	0-1

[5] Because the DIS measures were coded on a 0-1 scale, the mean indicates the percentage of study participants who report that they have engaged in the specified behavior.

Demographic Variables

I incorporate three standard demographic variables into the logistic regressions: age, level of education, ethnicity, and sex. I modified the measure of ethnicity, which initially included eight options, to create a bimodal variable. Since this data was collected in Bloomington, Indiana, the ethnic variation of the recruited pool of study participants is fairly limited. I thus code ethnicity as 0 (white) or 1 (non-white). Sex is coded as 0 (female) and 1 (male). Education and age were left as continuous variables.

Labeling

The DIS includes several questions that incorporate some measure of labeling theory. Labeling theory suggests that the more one is remarked upon by others as someone who does particular things or possesses certain characteristics, the more likely one is to incorporate and reify those characteristics within one's self. It seems plausible, then, that extensive application of negative labels upon an individual, i.e., delinquent or malcontent or troublemaker, might correlate with this person embracing and further enacting those behaviors (Lemert 1951).

Several of the items included in the DIS capture varying dimensions of labeling. In total, there are five items from the DIS that can be considered potential measures of the labeling process, as occurring during the childhood and teenage years. One in particular, DIS #19, seemed an appropriate measure for use in this study: "Were you ever arrested as a juvenile or sent to juvenile court?" Response options included "No," "Occasionally," and "Frequently." As with the other questions that listed

"No," "Occasionally," and "Frequently" response options, these response options were collapsed into a 0-1 construction for the purpose of analysis. This question seems to most overt and significant measure of labeling during the childhood/teen years (age 18 and younger) since it discriminates between those who have experienced official labeling and those who have not.

The Model

The basic form of the model used in the logistic regressions is as follows:

$$\log\left[\frac{\pi_i}{1 - \pi_i}\right] = \beta x_i$$

where π_i is the probability of adult fighting behavior for person i. The model is used to estimate the odds of adult fighting behavior for all study participants combined. β_j is the vector of regression parameters associated with the explanatory variables. The vector of explanatory variables (X_i) includes demographic variables such as age, education, and sex as well as the childhood/adolescent anti-social behavioral measures described above.

Supplemental Interview Data

I aspire to provide depth and texture to the broader quantitative findings with the interview data. In this portion of the study, I explore respondents' narrative accounts for explaining their relations with animals, both positive and negative. Some subjects may begin by identifying themselves as non-abusers but then, in the course of the interview, reassess this assertion. Others, even when confronted with the social demands of the interview environment, wherein the respondent is engaged in an explicit discussion of a past behavior and thereby forced to reconsider an act that might be deemed cruel, will resist such a designation.

As Weinberg et al.'s (1994) and others' (for example, Doug Pryor's [1996] study of men who sexually abuse children) work has suggested, sometimes the very engagement of such questions of identification during the interviewing process marks the first occasion at which a subject has overtly attempted to articulate their impressions of past events. For many subjects, this interview will mark the first time that they have carefully considered their

Table 3.3. *Interview Question Guide*

Interview Questions:
Did your family have any pets as you were growing up?   • How would you describe some of the relationships you've had with animals over the years?
What kinds of cruel things have you seen done to animals?
Who have you witnessed doing these sorts of things?   • If parents, probe as to the discipline employed within the household.

Please describe the most memorable incident of such cruelty that you have witnessed.
   • How old were you then?
   • What happened?

Please tell me about the kinds of cruel things you've done to animals?

(Table 3.3, cont.)

Did you do these things alone or in a group? •   <u>ALONE</u>: How did you tend to view the animal? What do you think caused you to do these things? •   <u>IN A GROUP</u>: What was the gender composition of the group? How did the typical incident start out?
Tell me about the most memorable incident you've participated in. Take me back to this event. . . •   How old were you? •   How many people participated? •   How many Men/Women? •   Had you/anyone else been drinking? •   Please tell me how the event unfolded? •   How did you feel before/during/after the incident? •   Did you feel any kind of thrill due to your participation? •   Why do you think you did what you did?
Tell me what you consider to have been the worst thing you have done to an animal. Take me back to this event. . . •   How old were you? •   How many people participated? •   How many Men/Women? •   Had you/anyone else been drinking? •   Please tell me how the event unfolded? •   How did you feel before/during/after the incident? •   Did you feel any kind of thrill due to your participation? •   Why do you think you did what you did?
What kinds of violent acts have you imagined doing to an animal?
What acts of violence have you imagined doing to another person? •   Have you ever acted on such inclinations/been in a physical altercation with another person? •   What, would you say, is the worst thing you have ever done to another person?

behavior toward animals with another person. The interview is designed to clarify (a) how the subject views him- or herself in relation to animals, (b) what patterns of human-animal interaction he or she may have learned in his or her family of origin, (c) the degree to which the subject feels alienated from other humans and/or compelled to act out in deviant ways, and (d) the meaning the subject infers upon any reported acts of cruelty.

The interview questions are open-ended and designed to clarify and augment the survey data. Because of the nature of my topic and the subjects recruited for the study, all of the questions or core concepts are asked at some point during the interview, though the ordering of questions may differ from interview to interview. Additionally, of course, probing may vary among interviews.

Interview data was examined using a grounded theory approach, succinctly summarized in Becker's (1990) article regarding generalizing from case studies and conceptual matrixes (Miles and Huberman 1994) to identify common themes given by interviewees by way of explaining why they had been cruel to animals. Additionally, efforts by interviewees to define or conceptualize cruelty were also examined for themes. Once themes were identified, code words were created to systematically search the transcribed text of the interviews using Nud*st qualitative data analysis software. This software was especially useful for search text based upon the logic of the matrixes, i.e., for searching for theoretically related key words and concepts occurring in close proximity to one another.

The next chapters (Chapter 4 and 5) reports upon my quantitative analyses, divided into two sets of hypotheses. The first set of hypotheses, reported in Chapter 4, discusses the basic question of whether or not there was any indication in these data that animal cruelty during childhood correlates with later adult violence. The second set of hypotheses, reported in Chapter 5, examine how reported rates of animal cruelty differ by sex and whether or not animal cruelty is more likely to lead to adult violence among men, in particular. The results of the qualitative interviews are indexed for themes, using the grounded theory approach, in Chapter 6.

CHAPTER IV

Does animal cruelty during childhood correlate with being violent toward humans later in life?

Here, I present the results of the analyses of my central hypotheses, that animal cruelty is (a) not a rare behavior, and (b) less associated with a violent or sociopathic trajectory than with a wide range of relatively minor anti-social infractions during adolescence. I begin by examining whether animal cruelty during childhood correlates with human-directed violence later in the life course, organizing my presentation by four hypotheses:

- Ho_1: Reports of animal abuse during the childhood or teenage years are not an especially unusual event— for instance, at least 1 in 10 individuals will report this behavior.

- Ho_2: Animal cruelty enacted during childhood/adolescence is more strongly correlated with other non-violent, anti-social behaviors rather than with violent anti-social behavior.

- Ho$_3$: Animal cruelty is not a strong predictor of future human-directed violence.

- Ho$_4$: Labeling theory more reliably predicts which individuals will carry anti-social behavioral tendencies into adulthood. Individuals who displayed anti-social, and especially violent, tendencies as children and were then *labeled* as deviant or delinquent during their formative years are especially likely to continue violent behavior into adulthood.

I examine each of these hypotheses, below. I first identify relevant patterns of anti-social behavior for my entire study group (N = 570) to address hypotheses 1-4.

Reported Involvement in Anti-Social Behavior

Descriptive data for the childhood and adolescent behavioral measures used to test these hypotheses explored in this study are reported in Table 4.1, below. There were 570 participants in this study group, and this first table presents the percentage of these 570 individuals who report having engaged in any of the identified anti-social behaviors.

Evident in Table 4.1 is that 14% of the sample reports having engaged in acts of animal cruelty as a child. Also interesting is that 25-35% or more of the study group report involvement as children in a range of other deviant acts—some as minimal as lying (38%) and some more serious, eg. fire-setting (27%), stealing (52%), vandalism (35%), and school suspension (26%). Of course, some individuals may very well have reported multiple acts, but, for this study, my focus is on the reported incidence of the acts

Table 4.1. *Percentage of Study Participants Reporting the Anti-Social Childhood/Adolescent Behavioral Measures Examined in this Study (N = 570)*

Measure	Percent Reporting Behavior during Childhood/Adolescence
DIS 2. IN TROUBLE AT SCHOOL When you were a child or teenager, did you frequently get into trouble with the teacher or principal for misbehaving in school?	29%
DIS 4. SUSPENDED Were you ever suspended from school?	26%
DIS 5. EXPELLED Were you ever expelled from school?	13%
DIS 7. FIGHTING Did you ever get in trouble with the police, your parents, or neighbors because of fighting (other than with siblings) outside of school?	19%
DIS 8. FIGHTING w/WEAPONS Did you ever use a weapon (like a stick, gun, or knife) in a fight?	8%
DIS 9. ANIMAL CRUELTY When you were a child or a teenager, were you ever mean or cruel to animals or did you intentionally hurt animals (mammals, not insects, etc.)?	14%
DIS 10. BULLYING When you were young, did people ever complain that you bullied or were mean to other children?	13%
DIS 11. HURTING SIBLINGS When you were a child or a teenager, did you ever intentionally hurt your siblings or other children seriously enough to cause notice by parents/surrogate?	20%
DIS 13. LYING Of course, no one tells the truth all of the time, but did you tell a lot of lies when you were a child or a teenager?	38%
DIS 15. STEALING When you were a child, did you more than once swipe things from stores or from other children, or steal from your parents or from anyone else?	52%

Table 4.1, cont.

DIS 17. VANDALISM
When you were a kid, did you ever intentionally (on purpose) damage
someone's car or house or do anything else to destroy someone else's
property?   35%

DIS 18. FIRESETTING
When you were a child or a teenager, did you ever set any fires you
were not supposed to?   27%

DIS 19. JUVENILE ARREST
Were you ever arrested as a juvenile or sent to juvenile court?   13%

---

themselves, not upon the characteristic types of individuals who might be performing these acts.

Thus, while not as common as behaviors such as lying, stealing, or fire-setting, animal cruelty is on a par with bullying and expulsion from school but more likely to be reported than fighting with weapons. Arguably, then, this confirms my first hypothesis, that animal cruelty is not an especially rare behavior.

The next question becomes one of examining the correlation between animal cruelty and these other anti-social behaviors.

Childhood/Adolescent Anti-Social Behaviors Associated with Animal Cruelty

In total, of the 570 subjects who participated in this study, 77 report having engaged in animal cruelty as children. All but five subjects also report engagement in other delinquent acts. My second hypothesis addresses an important question: does animal cruelty, perpetuated during the childhood or teenage years, associate more closely with other delinquent acts that are violent or with other delinquent acts that are non-violent? The role of animal cruelty in delinquent identity formation demands not only an examination of how animal cruelty during childhood or adolescence relates to adult behavior but also of how it correlates with other delinquent youth behaviors.

Table 4.2 (below) examines the extent to which animal cruelty correlates with other anti-social acts during childhood/adolescence. For each of the twelve reported behaviors, two breakdowns are provided: (a) the percentage of study participants who report engaging in the specified behavior but do not report engaging in animal cruelty and (b) the percentage of study participants who report engaging in the specified behavior and also report engaging in animal cruelty. By clarifying the overlap between study participants who report each of the specified behaviors and animal cruelty, these comparisons provide a clearer portrait of how extensively reports of involvement in each of the twelve other anti-social behaviors examined in this study correlate with reports of involvement in animal cruelty. Gammas and their significance levels are reported for the purpose of assessing the validity of these correlations. Note that the reported N varies by the measure being examined. For instance, while 116 study participants report hurting siblings, only 33 report being expelled from school.

From Table 4.2 it is evident that animal cruelty correlates with trouble at school (gamma = .48), fighting (gamma = .62), bullying (gamma = .60), hurting siblings (gamma = .53), stealing (gamma = .45), vandalizing (gamma = .68), fire setting (gamma = .62), and juvenile arrest6 (gamma = .50). In fact, animal cruelty significantly

---

[6] It should be noted that the juvenile arrest would not necessarily have been for an act of animal cruelty (with such arrests, though often high-profile, being rare).

Table 4.2. *Percentage of Subjects Reporting Engagement in Anti-Social Behaviors During Childhood/Adolescence, as Correlated to Animal Cruelty, Including Gammas and the N for Each Behavior Examined*

Measure	Percent Reporting This Behavior but NOT Animal Cruelty	Percent Reporting Both This Behavior AND Animal Cruelty	Gamma
In Trouble w/Principal (N=163)	76.7%	23.3%	.48***
Suspended from School (N=146)	79.5%	20.5%	.35**
Expelled from School (N=33)	66.7%	33.3%	.56*
Fighting (N=106)	68.9%	31.1%	.62***
Using Weapons (N=45)	68.9%	31.1%	.54**
Bullying (N=74)	67.5%	32.4%	.60***
Hurting Siblings (N=116)	73.3%	26.7%	.53***
Lying (N=216)	81.9%	18.1%	.29*
Stealing (N=294)	81.3%	18.7%	.45***
Vandalizing (N=200)	73.5%	26.5%	.68***
Fire-setting (N=155)	72.3%	27.7%	.62***
Juvenile Arrest (N=102)	73.5%	26.5%	.50***

*** p < .001   ** p < .01   * p < .05

correlates with all of these behaviors. Thus, there is little pattern evidenced in terms of the characterization of the clustering with regard to animal cruelty being violent or non-violent so that my second hypothesis is not confirmed.

Although various non-violent childhood and correlation with animal cruelty, there is a similar pattern of association between animal cruelty and reports of such violent acts as fighting (gamma = .62), bullying (gamma = .60), and hurting siblings (gamma = .53). One might argue that the non-violent behaviors such as trouble at school (gamma = .48), stealing (gamma = .45), and vandalizing (gamma = .68) may correlate only because they are so common, but lying is also quite common. It is reported by 38% of study participants (see Table 4.1), but its correlation here, though significant, is weak (gamma = .29). Also interesting is that fire setting, which, along with animal cruelty, is also considered a "sign" of sociopathy per McDonald's (1963) "triangle," is reported by 27% of study participants and shows a strong correlation with animal cruelty (gamma = .62). One would not likely count fire setting as a violent act, unless it were done with the intention of harming someone, but it certainly could be viewed as an aggressive act.

This bifurcated result suggests that there may be two broad patterns with regard to reported childhood/teenage behaviors: one that is characterized by an inclination to break a wide range of rules by engaging in both violent and non-violent anti-social behavior and another that is characterized by "thrill-seeking" behaviors but not by violent acts. Again, these patterns refer to acts, not individuals, since any individual study participant might have reported any number or combination of acts.

A factor analysis of the thirteen measures of childhood/adolescence deviance listed in Table 4.1, following the procedures outlined by Kim and Mueller (1979), suggests that all of these measures could be associated as one factor. More likely, though, as suggested by a principal components analysis, there are three components, the first of which has an Eigenvalue of 3.74 (explaining 28.76% of variance). The Eigenvalues for the second and third components fall precipitously: 1.15 (explaining 8.85% of variance) for component two and 1.24 (explaining 8.64% of variance) for component three. However, based upon the Kaiser criterion, Eigenvalues of 1 or more suggest the possibility of separate, unique factors. This suggests that the thirteen behaviors under consideration are characterized by three factors, one of which is very strong and two of which are weaker.

Examining the components matrices using Varimax rotation with Kaiser Normalization (Table 4.3), three factors are identified. The following table summarizes the factor loading on all of the items considered for each of the factors.

The factor loading pattern suggests that each of the three factors is characterized by a distinct loading of components. The first factor loads the school trouble variables most strongly, including getting into trouble at school, being suspended from school, and being expelled from school. Juvenile arrest also loads into this factor. The next factor loading is characterized by the human-directed aggression measures (fighting, bullying, and hurting siblings) but also includes animal cruelty. Curiously, fighting with weapons does not load on the second factor, nor does it load on any other factor. The final factor loads lying, stealing, vandalism and fire setting.

The factor analysis results suggest a disconfirmation of my second hypothesis in that animal cruelty explicitly loads, here, with violent behavioral components. However, Table 4.2 suggests mixed results, as it shows animal cruelty to be correlated with both violent and non-violent behaviors. Taken together, these two findings suggest that, at the very least, the relationship between animal cruelty and other childhood or teenage anti-social behaviors is neither evident nor simplistic.

Table 4.3. *Rotated Components Matrix, Based upon Varimax Rotation with Kaiser Normalization (Rotation Converged in 5 Iterations)*

Component	1	2	3
In Trouble at School	.61	.22	.32
Suspended	.77	.04	.21
Expelled	.73	.09	-.08
Fighting	.32	.52	.19
Fighting w/Weapons	.36	.21	.14
Animal Cruelty	-.02	.67	.15
Bullying	.31	.56	-.02
Hurting Siblings	.15	.58	-.03
Lying	.14	-.11	.74
Stealing	.19	.10	.72
Vandalizing	.15	.42	.55
Fire Setting	.06	.47	.50
Juvenile Arrest	.45	.23	.38
Eigenvalue (variance explained)	3.74 (28.76%)	1.15 (8.85%)	1.24 (8.64%)

The next question is whether animal cruelty, regardless of its contemporaneous affiliations during childhood or adolescence, predicts violent behavior during adulthood.

Is Animal Cruelty Predictive of Future Violence?

I employ two measures of adult violence: fighting and fighting with weapons. While 100 respondents report fighting as an adult, only 39 report using a weapon in a fight. It is not, unfortunately, especially reliable to do a logistic regression with such a small set of subjects (i.e., an N of 39), but I do not want to lose the information on study participants who report fighting with weapons as adults.

Hence, I create two dependent variables for use in these logistic regression models: (1) simple fighting as an adult, which 100 study participants report, and (2) a combination of those study participants reporting fighting and those reporting fighting with a weapon, of which there are 139 reports by a total 111 study participants (i.e., some participants reported both fighting and fighting use of a weapon in a fight). The logistic regression results for models run with each of these dependent variables prove very similar in their structural patterns, so I report herein the models using the combined measure as the dependent variable.

I use logistic regression to measure how well various factors predict the dependent variable, in this case fighting as an adult. Results are reported in Table 4.4, above. Note that, in reporting logistic regression results, I am reporting odds ratios, which are standardized to 1.0. That is, for values greater than 1.0, as I report in Table 4.3, there is an

Table 4.4. *Odds of Fighting or Fighting with a Weapon as an Adult as Predicted by Childhood/Adolescent Anti-Social Behaviors (Logistic Regression)*

DV: Fighting as an Adult	Model 1	Model 2	Model 3
Age	1.20**	1.19**	1.06
Education	.69***	.69***	.82
Gender (0 = females)			
Males	3.52***	3.18***	2.34**
Ethnicity (0 = whites)			
Non-whites	.39***	.38***	.48*
Animal Cruelty		1.99*	1.11
In Trouble w/Teacher			1.05
Suspended from School			1.91*
Expelled from School			1.81
Fighting			4.22***
Using Weapons			8.72***
Bullying			1.24
Hurting Siblings/Others			1.11
Lying			2.32**
Stealing			1.50
Vandalizing			1.50
Fire-setting			.47*
Log-likelihood	502.96	497.86	374.55
Degrees of freedom	4	5	16
Number of cases	570	570	570

***p≤.001   **p≤.01   *p≤.05

increase in odds. For values less than 1.0, there is a decrease in odds. Hence, 1.19 suggests a 19% increase in the likelihood of the outcome of the dependent variable, in this case fighting behavior. Alternatively, .81 would suggest a 19% decrease in the likelihood of the outcome of the dependent variable.

Within Model 1, each demographic variable shows a relationship to fighting as an adult. For each additional year of age, an individual is 20% more likely (p < .01) to report fighting as an adult. Recall, though, that the mean age of this sample population is quite low (20.72) so that it is likely that the predictive trajectory of age would wane, even reversing itself as this population ages. Several studies, most notably Gottfredson and Hirschi (1990) and Sampson and Laub (1995), have found that the propensity toward criminality and anti-social behavior more generally diminishes as one progress through the life course.

For each additional year of education, one is 31% less likely (p < .001) to report fighting as an adult. Men are 252% more likely (p < .001) to report fighting as an adult than are women. Non-whites are 61% less likely (p < .001) to report fighting as an adult than are whites, which is perhaps explained by the small number of non-whites in this sample and the likelihood that those non-whites who did participate are more likely to be more highly educated than their peers.

In Model 2, I add the measure of animal cruelty to the demographic variables and find that individuals who reported abusing animals as children or teenagers are 99% more likely (p < .05) than those who did not report abusing animals to report fighting as an adult. Each of the demographic variables remains significant in this model, as well.

In Model 3, I add the other measures of childhood/teenage anti-social behavior and find that the effect of animal abuse disappears. In this model, education, gender, and ethnicity remain significant. Reporting to have fought, used weapons, or lied as a child also evidences highly significant explanatory power. Those who report fighting as a child/teenager were 322% more likely (p < .001) to have report fighting as an adult than those who did not report fighting as a child or teenager. Those who report using weapons in fights as a child/adolescent were 772% more likely (p < .001) to report having gotten into fights as an adult than are those who do not. Finally, those who report having lied routinely as a child/teenager were 132% more likely (p < .01) to report fighting as an adult than those who had not reported lying regularly as a child/teenager. Here, again, it is interesting that animal cruelty is not associated with adult violence once we control for other childhood/teenage behaviors. Still, violent behaviors such as bullying are also not associated with adult violence. It is behaviors such as lying, fire setting, and being suspended from school that are more strongly associated with adult violence.

These are intriguing results, which support my third hypothesis that being cruel to animals, as a child or teenager, does not render one more likely to engage in violent behavior as an adult. Though animal cruelty does show predictive power in Model 2, it does not show predictive power net of other childhood/teenage anti-social behaviors. When we combine the full range of deviant childhood or adolescent behaviors, we find that there are a few key behaviors associated with fighting as an adult and that animal cruelty is not one of them. Interestingly, neither are some violent behaviors such as bullying.

The next table, Table 4.5, examines the possibility that animal cruelty may drop out of significance because so many other terms are included in Model 3. I test this possibility, below, by running logistic regression models based upon the factor analysis presented earlier, in which three distinct factors were evidenced. The components of the first factor included trouble at school, suspension from school, expulsion from school, and juvenile arrest. The second factor loaded fighting, bullying, and hurting siblings. The third incorporated lying, stealing, vandalism, and fire setting. These models permit the ability to test the relationship of these different sets of variables against animal cruelty.

Table 4.5 reports three models, the first of which uses the first factor's components plus the measure of animal cruelty. The second and third models follow a similar pattern, using the components from factors two and three as independent variables for models two and three, respectively. As in Model 1, the second and third models also include the measure of animal cruelty.

The results of the assessment presented in Table 4.5 suggest that there are some interesting complexities within this data. Though animal cruelty loads as a significant component upon the second factor proposed by the factor analysis, it is not significant at all in any of the models shown in Table 4.5. In the first model, outside of the demographic variables, suspension and expulsion are significant predictors of adult anti-social behavior. In the second model, only fighting is significant, beyond the demographic variables. Finally, in the third model, lying, stealing, and vandalism are significant. All of the demographic variables except age[7] are significant across the models, with gender having the most consistent and sizable impact upon adult violence. Animal cruelty consistently drops out of significance even when considered against relatively minor, non-aggressive items

---

[7] Education is actually not significant in the first model, but this is likely only because the model incorporates several specific measures of school behavior.

Table 4.5. *Odds of Fighting or Fighting with a Weapon as an Adult as Predicted by Youth Anti-Social Behaviors, Models Derived from Factor Analysis Results (Logistic Regression)*

DV: Fighting as an Adult	Model 1	Model 2	Model 3
Age	1.06	1.13	1.17
Education	.87	.74***	.74***
Gender (0 = females)			
Males	2.70***	2.56***	2.66**
Ethnicity (0 = whites)			
Non-whites	.38***	.35***	.39*
Animal Cruelty	1.79	1.42	1.68
In Trouble w/Teacher	1.55		
Suspended from School	2.83***		
Expelled from School	2.41*		
Fighting		5.07***	
Using Weapons			
Bullying		1.64	
Hurting Siblings/Others		1.37	
Lying			2.38***
Stealing			1.83*
Vandalizing			2.19**
Fire-setting			.80
Juvenile Arrest	1.34		
Log-likelihood	452.19	444.87	453.15
Degrees of freedom	9	8	9
Number of cases	570	570	570

***p≤.001   **p≤.01   *p≤.05

like the educational measures of "trouble at school" or "suspension from school." One might expect animal cruelty to drop out of significance when considered against fighting as a child/teenager, but it falls out of significance in all combinations of variables.

The question now becomes: what factors, if any, might do better than animal cruelty in predicting violent tendencies in adulthood? One guess might be that being labeled violent or anti-social during childhood might be a good predictor of violence later in life.

Labeling Theory and Animal Cruelty

The next step is to assess the impact that labeling processes might have upon adult anti-social behavioral outcomes. I demonstrated earlier that study participants reporting animal cruelty are also likely to report a range of other anti-social behaviors. According to labeling theory, if someone is inclined to break the rules, it is likely that he or she will be much more likely to break the rules once he or she is officially labeled a "troublemaker" or "deviant."

This idea is consonant with the pattern of correlation between study participants who report both being arrested or having had to go to court as a juvenile and the other reported anti-social behaviors. Table 4.6 illustrates these correlation patterns.

Here we see that study participants who report having been arrested or forced to appear in court as children were much more likely to have been engaged in a range of anti-social enterprises. They are especially more likely to report having had encounters with authority figures at school, i.e., to have gotten in trouble with teachers and principals (gamma = .71) or to have been suspended (gamma = .67) or expelled (gamma = .73) from school. These individuals are

Table 4.6. *Percentage of Subjects Reporting Engagement in Anti-Social Behaviors During Childhood/Adolescence, as Correlated to Juvenile Arrest or Court Appearance (N for Each Behavior Reported in Parentheses), Gammas Reported*

Measure	Percent Reporting ONLY the Behavior Listed at Left	Percent Reporting BOTH this Behavior AND Juvenile Arrest or Court Appearance	Gamma
In Trouble w/Principal (N=163)	61.3%	38.7%	.71***
Suspended from School (N=146)	61.6%	38.4%	.67***
Expelled from School (N=33)	45.5%	54.5%	.73***
Fighting (N=106)	59.4%	40.6%	.65***
Using Weapons (N=45)	66.7%	33.3%	.43*
Animal Cruelty (N = 77)	64.9%	35.1%	.50***
Bullying (N=74)	62.2%	37.8%	.55***
Hurting Siblings (N=116)	70.7%	29.3%	.40**
Lying (N=216)	73.6%	26.4%	.42***
Stealing (N=294)	73.5%	26.5%	.53***
Vandalizing (N = 200)	66.5%	33.5%	.66***
Fire-setting (N=155)	66.5%	33.5%	.57***

also particularly more likely to report fighting (gamma = .65) or vandalism (gamma = .66). Also, because there is no longitudinal dimension to this data during the childhood/teenage years, i.e., given that all the data is based upon retrospective reporting by adults, it is impossible to know whether the official labeling was a causative factor in the behavior or solely a consequence. All that can be said for certain is that there is correlation between this measure of labeling and several of the other childhood/adolescent behaviors.

The next step, then, is to assess the impact that labeling processes might have upon adult anti-social behavioral outcomes. The following table (Table 4.7) adds a fourth and fifth model to Table 4.4, so as to incorporate the dimension of labeling, as measured by arrest or court appearance as a juvenile, into the logistic regression model. Model 4 considers the measure of labeling on its own. Model 5 includes an interaction term for labeling and animal cruelty, to gauge the impact of the interaction of labeling and animal cruelty upon future adult fighting behavior.

Here we see that, in Model 4, the explanatory power of several variables that were significant in Model 3 remains rather stable. In fact, there seems little evidence here that labeling processes, as measured here, have any significant effect on adult fighting outcomes. The most significant childhood/adolescent behaviors remain fighting, which increases the odds that one will fight as an adult by more than 300% in both Model 4 and 5 (p < .001), and fighting with weapons, which increases the odds of one reporting fighting as an adult by nearly 800% (p < .001).

Table 4.7. *Odds of Fighting or Fighting with a Weapon as an Adult as Predicted by Youth Anti-Social Behaviors, Including Labeling Measures (Logistic Regression)*

DV: Fighting as Adult	Model 1	Model 2	Model 3	Model 4	Model 5
Age	1.20**	1.19**	1.06	1.06	1.06
Education	.69***	.69***	.82	.82	.82
Gender	3.52***	3.18***	2.34**	2.34**	2.31**
Ethnicity	.39***	.38***	.48**	.48*	.47*
Animal Cruelty		1.99*	1.11	1.11	1.44
Fighting			4.22***	4.23***	4.24***
Using Weapons			8.72***	8.70***	8.47***
Bullying			1.24	1.24	1.26
Hurting Siblings/Others			1.11	1.11	1.09
Lying			2.32**	2.31**	2.35**
Stealing			1.50	1.50	1.50
Vandalizing			1.50	1.50	1.49
Fire-setting			.47*	.47*	.46*
In Trouble at School			1.05	1.05	1.05
Suspended from School			1.91*	1.92*	1.89*
Expelled from School			1.81	1.82	1.81
Labeling				.98	1.12
Interaction of Labeling & Animal Cruelty					.54
Log likelihood	502.96	497.86	374.55	374.55	373.66
Degrees of freedom	4	5	16	17	18
# of cases	570	570	570	570	570

***p≤.001   **p≤.01   *p≤.05

In Model 5, I add the labeling interaction term to the model, and this also produces no significant results. The measure of labeling shows no significance, nor does the interaction term. Again, the structure evidenced in Models 3 and 4 is retained in Model 5, with fighting during childhood/adolescence and using weapons during childhood/adolescence being the best predictors of adult fighting. These results suggest that I must reject my eigth hypothesis. I had hypothesized with my fourth hypothesis, that labeling forces might affect the probability that one might engage in fighting behavior as an adult, but this did not prove to be the case. Fighting and fighting with weapons remain the only variables that show strong predictive power.

Conclusions

At the very least, my results suggest that the conventional wisdom arguing that animal cruelty enacted during childhood or adolescence leads to human-directed violence later in life is not well-supported by these data. These quantitative data confirm some of my hypotheses but disconfirm others. With regard to the first hypothesis, that animal cruelty is not a particularly unusual event, there is evident confirmation for this hypothesis, particularly when considering men. About 14% of the total study population reports animal abuse, but a full 22% of the men report animal cruelty.

The second hypothesis, that animal cruelty is more correlated during the childhood/teenage years with non-violent anti-social behaviors, is not clearly confirmed. Examining the correlation matrix for animal cruelty and each of the other childhood/teenage behaviors (Table 4.2), one notes that animal cruelty correlates with all of the other behaviors. Examining the factor analysis results, however, it is evident that animal cruelty factors with the violent anti-social childhood/teenage behaviors.

The third hypothesis is confirmed. Animal abuse very consistently shows no correlation with adult human-directed violence once other measures of childhood/adolescent anti-social behavior are incorporated into the model. Though animal cruelty may, in some ways, be associated with violent behaviors, this correlation is quite complicated.

Finally, the fourth hypothesis must be rejected. Labeling theory provides no better explanation of tendencies toward violence as an adult than does animal cruelty enacted during childhood.

CHAPTER V

How do women's and men's reported rates of animal cruelty differ?

One level of inquiry that seems worth pursuing is that of gender. The roles and labels that we internalize are strongly driven by gender. Thus, I explore here the interplay of gender and anti-social behavior in these data. It seems plausible that there are distinct differences between men and women in the prevalence, meaning, and enactment of animal cruelty and other forms of anti-social behavior. I consider three hypotheses, which incorporate ideas extending from theories exploring the intersections of gender and deviance:

- Ho_5: Men are more likely than women to report having engaged in an act of animal cruelty during their formative years, i.e., when they were a child or teenager.

- Ho_6: Overall, men are more likely to be officially labeled as deviant than are women.

- Ho$_7$: Animal cruelty, though more commonly reported among men, nonetheless shows no correlation with reports of adult violence among men.

An examination of the logistic regression models explored in the previous sections will likely evidence stronger, clearer patterns once the dimension of gender is considered. In terms of being able to calculate odds ratios for the adult outcome of fighting behavior, however, I am relegated to running a men-only model because there are so few women who report fighting as an adult (i.e., there are insufficient numbers to run a stable logistic regression model).

Many More Men than Women Report Having Engaged in Animal Cruelty

The study participant population includes 282 men and 288 women. Responding to the query, "When you were a child or a teenager, were you ever mean or cruel to animals or did you intentionally hurt animals (mammals, not insects, etc.)?" just 5% of women answered yes (with a standard deviation of .215), while 22% of men answered that they had (S.D. = .417).

Table 5.1 presents the incidence of various forms of deviance by gender and presents chi-square data, which indicates whether there is a significant difference between the sexes in terms of the listed behavior.

The difference between men and women with regard to their involvement in animal cruelty was highly significant (chi-square = 30.79 with 1 degree of freedom; p < .001). Therefore in terms of Ho$_5$, I can reasonably conclude that, not only do a sizeable number of men report engaging in animal cruelty, but men's reported involvement in this

Table 5.1. *Descriptive Statistics for the Anti-Social Behavioral Measures Used in this Study, by Gender (N = 570) with Chi-squares Reported (Degrees of freedom in Parentheses)*

Measure	Pctg. of Men Reporting Behavior During Childhood/ Adolescence (N = 282)	Pctg. of Women Reporting Behavior During Childhood/ Adolescence (N = 288)	Chi-square (df = 1)
DIS 2. *In Trouble at School*	36.9%	20.5%	18.75***
DIS 4. *Suspended*	30.9%	20.5%	8.03**
DIS 5. *Expelled*	8.5%	3.1%	7.58**
DIS 7. *Fighting*	27.3%	10.1%	27.96***
DIS 8. *Fighting w/Weapons*	13.1%	2.8%	20.96***
DIS 9. *Animal Cruelty*	22.3%	4.9%	30.79***
DIS 10. *Bullying*	14.9%	11.1%	1.81
DIS 11. *Hurting Siblings*	25.2%	15.6%	8.02**
DIS 13. *Lying*	40.4%	35.4%	1.52
DIS 15. *Stealing*	58.5%	44.8%	10.74***
DIS 17. *Vandalism*	51.8%	18.8%	68.22***
DIS 18. *Firesetting*	46.1%	8.7%	100.76**
DIS 19. *Juvenile Arrest*	23.4%	12.5%	11.53**

***p≤.001   **p≤.01   *p≤.05

behavior is significantly more common than is that of women's reported involvement. It also becomes evident, looking at Table 5.1, that several other childhood/teenage anti-social behaviors can also be distinguished in terms of gender. In fact, only bullying and lying do not demonstrate a significant difference in terms of the reported involvement by men and women. Finally, per Ho_6, men are twice as likely as women to be officially labeled a deviant, with 23.4% of men reporting juvenile arrest and only 12% of women reporting the same (chi-square = 11.53 with 1 degree of freedom; p < .01).[8]

Logistic Analysis of How Animal Cruelty Affects Adult Fighting Behavior, Considered for Men

The logistic regression analysis is again limited by the number of cases available where study participants report adult fighting behavior ("fighting as an adult" and "using weapons as an adult" are again considered as a combined category). With only 30 women in the study reporting fighting as an adult and only 8 reporting use of weapons, there are insufficient numbers of women to perform a reliable logistic regression to examine adult outcomes of women's behaviors in terms of childhood/adolescent involvement in animal cruelty.

However, with regard to men, there are a total of 80 men who report fighting and/or using weapons in a fight as an adult. Thus, this section examines logistic models for

---

[8] Note: an analysis such as that reported in Table 4.2 (above), in which I examined the extent to which reported animal cruelty correlated with other anti-social behaviors, is not advisable with regard to comparing men with women because women comprise only 14 of the 77 study participants who report engaging in animal cruelty.

men only so as to address the ninth and tenth hypotheses. The following model replicates Tables 4.4 and 4.5 into a combined table reporting for men only.

Table 5.2, below, demonstrates very similar patterns to those found in Tables 4.4 and 4.5, which is not particularly surprising given that most of the study participants who report engaging in fighting as an adult are men.

What is evident in Models 1 and 2 is that education is the only demographic variable that is significant. For every year of education, one has a 23-24% less chance of engaging in fighting behavior as an adult. In Model 2, animal cruelty is significant, suggesting that having abused animals renders one 100% more likely to engage in fighting behavior as an adult. As in the earlier models (4.4 and 4.5), however, this correlation subsides as other measures of childhood/teenage anti-social behavior are added to Model 3. Consistent across Models 3, 4, and 5, engaging in fighting behavior or using weapons in a fight as a child most dramatically increases one's odds of fighting as an adult.

The labeling measure again proves inconsequential when introduced in Model 4. Even after the interaction term for animal abuse crossed with labeling is introduced, the basic structure of the model remains unfettered. Fighting as a child, and especially fighting with weapons as a child remains the strongest predictor of fighting as an adult.

These results confirms my seventh hypothesis, suggesting that animal cruelty indeed offers no reliable prediction of adult violent behavior in men.

Table 5.2 *Men's Odds of Fighting or Fighting with a Weapon as an Adult as Predicted by Youth Anti-Social Behaviors (Logistic Regression)*

DV: Fighting as an Adult	Model 1	Model 2	Model 3	Model 4	Model 5
Age	1.13	1.13	1.07	1.07	1.08
Education	.76**	77**	.85	.85	.83
Ethnicity (0 = whites)					
Non-whites	.57	.53	.52	.54	.53
Animal Cruelty		2.00*	1.09	1.09	1.52
Fighting			3.99***	4.05***	4.15***
Using Weapons			7.79***	7.78***	7.39***
Bullying			1.55	1.58	1.65
Hurting Siblings/Others			1.07	1.06	1.04
Lying			1.53	1.54	1.57
Stealing			1.24	1.25	1.29
Vandalizing			1.40	1.41	1.39
Fire-setting			.51	.52	.52
In Trouble w/Teacher			1.07	1.10	1.11
Suspended from School			1.58	1.60	1.51
Expelled from School			1.29	1.33	1.31
Labeling				.81	1.17
Interaction of Labeling & Animal Cruelty					.29
Log-likelihood	326.69	321.80	250.88	250.76	248.37
Degrees of freedom	1	4	15	16	17
Number of cases	282	282	282	282	282

***$p \leq .001$ **$p \leq .01$ *$p \leq .05$

The following table, Table 5.3, examines the dimension of labeling not as a predictive factor but as a variable that might be correlated with other anti-social behaviors. This replicates Table 4.7, above, but considers these correlations for men and then women.

Table 5.3 illustrates that, among men, many of the childhood/teenage anti-social behaviors correlate with labeling, as measured by juvenile arrest. In particular, getting into trouble at school (gamma = .77), suspension from school (gamma = .72), expulsion from school (gamma = .74), fighting (gamma = .65), bullying (gamma = .66), and vandalism (gamma = .66) show an especially strong correlation with juvenile arrest or court appearance.

Table 5.3. *Percentage of Study Participants Reporting Both the Listed Childhood/Adolescent Behavior (X) and Juvenile Arrest (JA), by Sex (gammas reported in parentheses)*

MEASURE	MEN				WOMEN			
	N	Only X	JA+X	Gamma	N	Only X	JA+X	Gamma
In Trouble w/Teacher or Principal	104	53.8%	46.2%	.77***	59	74.6%	25.4%	.54**
Suspended from School	87	52.9%	47.1%	.72***	59	74.6%	25.4%	.54**
Expelled from School	24	37.5%	62.5%	.74***	9	66.7%	33.3%	.58
Fighting	77	54.5%	45.5%	.65**	29	72.4%	27.6%	.52*
Using Weapons in Fights	37	59.5%	40.5%	.44*	8	100%	0%	-1.00**
Animal Cruelty	63	76.6%	23.4%	.36*	14	87.5%	12.5%	.63
Bullying	42	47.6%	52.4%	.66***	32	81.3%	18.7%	.27
Hurting Siblings	71	62.0%	38.0%	.46**	45	84.4%	15.6%	.15
Lying	114	66.7%	33.3%	.43**	102	81.4%	18.6%	.39*
Stealing	165	68.5%	31.5%	.54***	129	79.8%	20.2%	.57***
Vandalizing	146	64.4%	35.6%	.66***	54	72.2%	28.8%	.59**
Fire-setting	130	66.2%	33.8%	.50***	25	68.0%	32.0%	.60*

For women, fire setting (gamma = .60), getting in trouble at school (gamma = .54), suspension (gamma = .54), fighting (gamma = .52), stealing (gamma = .57), and vandalism (gamma = .59) all demonstrate a significant correlation with juvenile arrest. Use of weapons as a child shows a completely negative correlation with juvenile arrest among women.

These patterns suggest that men who are labeled as children present a wider range of behaviors that correlate with their being labeled. For women, the behaviors showing the strongest correlation with juvenile arrest are fire setting, vandalism, and stealing. Again, of course, it is impossible to tell whether the study participants who report labeling were labeled for the specific behavior(s) that show correlation with labeling.

Conclusions

With regard to my hypotheses specific to gender, I find that men are indeed quite a bit more likely than women to report having engaged in an act of animal cruelty during their formative years (Ho_5). Additionally, men are much more likely to be officially labeled deviant than are women (Ho_6). Per Table 5.1, men are nearly twice as likely to have experienced juvenile arrest as are women. Also, as reported in Table 5.3, juvenile arrest correlates with a much wider array of behaviors for men than it does for women. Thus, confirming Ho_7, animal cruelty is no more predictive of adult human-directed violence for men than it is for the combined group of men and women, which is not surprising given that it is mostly men that report fighting behavior as adults. Labeling theory also shows no predictive power with regard to adult violence when considering men only, causing me to reject Ho_8. The logistic regression results' structure is almost identical between the analysis done on the entire study population and those done for men only. This is likely because it is largely men who report having engaged in animal cruelty.

CHAPTER VI:

Telling Tales to Account for Incidents of Animal Cruelty

Introduction

In addition to examining the 570 cases discussed above, I also interviewed 21 of the subjects included in these 570 cases about their experiences with animals and animal cruelty. I interviewed nearly an even number of men (N = 12) and women (N = 9). Specifically, I had the chance to speak with quite a few of the women who acknowledged having abused an animal in their DIS interviews. Since reports of animal abuse are relatively rare among women, I was especially interested in talking with admitted abusers who were female. I sought a mix of respondents, overall, however, some who had admitted to abusing animals in their DIS interview and some who did not. Also, I talked with some study participants who were classified as having Anti-Social Personality Disorder (the adult extension of Conduct Disorder, per the DSM-IV [1994]), and I talked with some study participants who were not so-classified.

Curiously, I interviewed six individuals who were classified as ASP and who responded to the initial DIS questions about previous animal cruelty with a negative response, suggesting they had never abused an animal. Three of these subjects were women and three were men. Of these three men, however, only one, in fact, maintained throughout the interview that he had never abused an animal. The other two remembered during the course of the interview that they had engaged in some act of cruelty as a child. All three of these ASP women who answered "No" to DIS Question #9 maintained throughout the interview that they had never abused an animal.

Because of the small number of interview respondents, I am disinclined to draw any grand conclusions from the qualitative data. I view this chapter more as a hypothesis-generating enterprise than as an effort to confirm or disconfirm any particular hypothesis as to how and why people might abuse animals. There has been relatively little open-ended interviewing of people— particularly non-incarcerated individuals and non-student populations (as were used in Arluke [2002])— regarding their abuse of animals. Hence, any data collected at this point will necessarily serve as a heuristic guide to future inquiry.

Each interview lasted from 1 - 2.5 hours, so I gathered information on quite a number of actual incidents of animal abuse, since some study participants described more than one such incident to me. This presentation of my data will mainly focus upon three matters: (1) factors involved in the way interviewees talk about their abusive episodes; (2) differences in the character of men's and women's acts of animal cruelty; and (3) an exploration of the process by which an individual might cease to abuse animals.

Factors Involved in Animal Abuse Incidents

In examining the accounts that study participants offered by way of explaining their abusive acts, I am struck not only by the themes that characterized these accounts but also by the effort on the part of interviewees to define cruelty. In a number of cases, interviewees attempt to glean from me some sense of whether or not an act they had described was really cruel, asking for instance, "Isn't that horrible?" or "That's not so cruel, is it?"

In terms of the themes that characterize the accounts given in explaining abusive acts, three particular concepts emerged. First, many interviewees articulate some version of the idea that they were bored, possibly drunk, and simply looking for something "fun" to do. Next, some accounts seem to orient themselves around a theme of justified violence, i.e., violence effected toward an animal as a way of getting back at someone, such as the owner of the animal, or, alternatively, expressing some more generalized frustration. Finally, some accounts seemed to illustrate an impetus to discipline animals, often in the same way that the respondent him or herself might have been disciplined by his or her parents.

Many study participants reported that they had engaged in acts of animal abuse as a part of a group of, usually, men (or, more specifically, boys). The following excerpts illustrate how these events typically unfolded. The following excerpt is from an account in which a respondent describes launching bottle rocket firecrackers at neighborhood cats:

> You got to have an idea of how long it (a bottle rocket) is going to take before it blows up. Depending if you want it to blow up next to or not

> next to the animal [sic]. But a lot of the time the
> bottle rocket will just screech by [and] will scare
> them [the animal] to death anyway. Mostly it's just
> the reaction. Jumps in the air and hair all poofs out
> and takes out [sic] running.

In this account, it is evident that the main attraction to doing such a thing is the reaction generated in the animal. In effect, the reaction seems comical to the young perpetrators: the hair "all poofs out," as it might in a cartoon. Another respondent recounted having spray-painted a neighborhood cat while drinking with some friends. As he tells it, "we were hanging out, drinking, and there was a cat and there was a can of spray paint and it just went from there." What happens from there is that the respondent and his friends go on to spray the cat with paint, just because it was something to do. Another respondent describes roaming about the neighborhood with a friend in the evenings and grabbing cats to toss into neighbors' pools: "it was hilarious— that cats would just freak out."

Sometimes, interviewees attempt to moderate the perceived harm or negative dimensions of their actions by noting that their acts had "not caused any terrible harm." Several study participants try to rationalize an act as "not that cruel," for instance: "we would tease the dog, but not really anything cruel." In many such cases, there seems to be an effort at forging a distinction between causing physical harm and "just teasing," which is more likely inclined toward some sort of emotional torment. In one such case, the participant claims that he "never really did anything to animals" but then remarks in the very next breath that, "I've swung a cat around by the tail." He also notes that he "shot at a horse" and had "thrown cats up in the air" and "into the pool," though he had, "never tried to hold them underwater or anything like that." In such cases, it seems as though the respondents are either not in fact sure an act was "cruel" or perhaps feel slightly bad about or embarrassed about some act done much earlier in life. I noticed an obvious effort by some respondents to frame, or account for, their behavior— and to test my reaction to the behavior they were sharing with me. The effort to cast an act as "not that bad" seems a way of negating the harm of such actions and, by extension, the actor. Sometimes, too, respondents will make distinctions between what they seem to deem as mischief and "real" cruelty. For instance, as in the previous quote, a respondent might consider tossing a cat into a pool to be funny and mischievous but not really cruel, as would be something like trying to drown the cat.

Alternatively, other respondents rationalize that there was simply nothing for them to do in their neighborhoods, as if they were left little choice but to wreak havoc on animals. Telling of his motivations for stalking neighborhood cats and throwing them into swimming pools, one respondent observes:

> There was just nothing to do. It was so boring. So, we'd go around and just walk around the neighborhood and we'd find something to do. It was fun with a cat or something because it'd run and you'd get to chase it. And there was some excitement because it'd scratch at you and it wasn't that easy to grab it.

Another respondent, in this case a female, recounts driving solo and trying to run over an animal:

> Yah, a couple of times I have [tried to hit an animal while driving]. Just to see if I could do it. You know, just for my, my curiosity kind of thing, you

know, but...um...in those incidents I never really
hit the animal either, even though I tried [laughing].

Such accounts seem to most strongly the idea that these
abusers are seeking— and finding— some sort of fun or
distraction in their acts.

An interesting illustration of how the violent treatment
of animals might provide some sort of intense
"entertainment," in effect "something to do" came from a
few subjects who appropriated the idea of "mercy killing"
an injured animal but yet evidenced a strong enjoyment of
this killing in their account of it. Describing an incident
wherein he had "mercy killed" a cat whose head had
accidentally been slammed inside a car door, the
respondent explains:

> Well, we didn't tell people for awhile cause we
> didn't know what they would say, you know, they
> were like, 'where's the cat at.' We're like, well, we
> had an accident. They were like I can't believe you
> all did that. It's like we didn't do it on purpose.
> And they're like how'd you step on its head? Well,
> I had to do something to it. But they're like, well
> how could you step on its head? Like. . . it was
> laying there dying, I mean [laugh], I helped it by
> steppin' on it's head b/c I mean it wasn't gonna to
> live [laugh]. I mean its head was smashed in
> [laugh], so. . .

This individual clearly understands that his acts might be
frowned upon by his peers— particularly female peers.
However, he also seems to find some amusement, or
entertainment, from "helping" the animal to die. Hence,
killing the animal is ostensibly done so as to put the animal

out of its misery, but the legitimized, or rationalized, use of such aggression is also enjoyed.

Another interviewee describes several incidents of "mercy killing" animals. Here, it seems as though this individual is experiencing some sort of an intense pleasure from these acts. Consider:

> These are kinda humane, in a sense they're humane acts, but umm. I can remember once. . . I can remember thrcc times I've killed an animal with my hands in the last few years. Once a squirrel ran in front of my car; I knew I hit it. But it ran off—it ran off no problem. But I caught it. It broke, it had a broken leg, and I, I just thought, well, I'm not gonna be setting the squirrel's [laugh] leg, so I just, you know, I grabbed it—I had gloves on, fortunately—I grabbed it by a hind leg, and I just hit it's head against the—a— log and blood sprayed everywhere and it died instantaneously. For me that was kinda being humane; other people [laugh] may well disagree.

A common tactic, exemplified here, is to attribute intention or purpose, thereby shifting blame, to the animal: "a squirrel ran in front of my car." Note as well the extent to which this respondent questions how humane his actions really are— it is as if he is trying to convince himself, which is interesting since many people would probably condone killing an animal that one had accidentally run over so as to put it out of its misery. The respondent, though, seems to realize that he may be taking some pleasure in these killings, which would surely not be condoned by most of his average, American adult

counterparts— again, particularly female peers. The study
participant continues:

> Another circumstance similar— someone else hit a
> rabbit; I didn't. But, I saw it on the side of the road
> and it was kickin' around—it wasn't dead yet, and
> so I stopped. And I tried to wring it's neck. What a
> mistake that was. A rabbit's neck is incredibly
> flexible, so I twisted it around [laugh] I could hear
> all these bones and sinews poppin,' and I all the
> way around and then I let go and it wasn't dead
> [laugh]. I couldn't believe it. I had to like do it
> twice and it was like ickkkk—get away from me.
> Throw it away, and like oh man, that was really. . .

Here, he admits that he has gone out of his way at times to
"end the suffering" of an animal that he did not even
himself injure.   And, again, the emphasis given to the
physical and emotional experience of killing this creature
implies the respondent's pleasure.   Though he indicates
being repulsed or disgusted, the detail he provides in this
account suggests a rather primal enjoyment of an act
wrapped within a thin veneer of rationalization.

Even this sort of abuse arguably mimics the sort of
reasoning that may motivate at least some incidents of
vandalism. As one respondent puts it:

> My cousin and I actually hung out with this other
> guy and together we would go to people's houses
> and torment cats and stuff like that. Actually, I still
> hang out with him quite a bit, and now we focus on
> other people. So, it's like we shifted from no
> animals, to animals, to other people. The animals
> weren't doing anything to me. But now, we don't
> have the money and don't really feel we can go to

school. And we're sitting around with friends and a group of guys that look like frat guys go walking by or frat girls walking by and we would yell things at them. It's jealousy. And sometimes it becomes fighting, or we might follow them and trash their cars later.

In this case, the interviewee is evidently effecting vandalism in the same way that some of the other respondents are engaging in animal cruelty, as a way of relieving frustration.

Other respondents seem to be motivated by factors, such as frustration, as well. One of the interviewees, for instance, extensively detailed his aggression toward a high school girlfriend's pet rabbit. The respondent felt that the girlfriend paid too much attention to the rabbit and cared too intently about it. He became jealous of her affection for the rabbit, feeling that she did not care enough for him:

I just hated the rabbit because it was, it was like uh, instead of spending time, I'd be like, hey why don't you come over here. Well, I'm gonna hang out with the rabbit, you know, and we're gonna. . . cuz she was so into this rabbit like, seriously, if it was a choice between my life and the rabbit's life, she would totally have to sit there and, I dunno. So, like I had such a problem with this rabbit that it was just like I would just hit it whenever I would see it. And she paid more attention to the rabbit.

This individual became so frustrated with the rabbit that he would spend significant amounts of time fantasizing how to hurt or kill it:

I hated it; it was almost like she was going out with someone, you know, someone else. I was thinking to myself at the time that I wanted to nail it to the wall and like split it open or something; I was also crazy at the time. And I wanted to do something to it but I didn't want her to know that I had anything to do with it, and it just kinda worked out that way. Like if I could do something like set it on fire and then like cross the wires on the washing machine so that would catch on fire so it'd look he chewed through the wires or something. I would just be totally down for that, if I wasn't worried about the ramifications of the house burning down.

Eventually, he resorted to hurting the rabbit one day when the girlfriend left it in his care:

I basically dropped it [the rabbit] and umm it was scratching me so I picked it up and I was telling it, umm, I think I was telling it how much I hated it or something [laugh]. And it was like scratching at my hand, and you know, I dropped it, and it broke its arm. [Prompt: *Did you just drop it?*9] It was a drop, but it was an intentional drop. I actually took it to the vet, you know—acted like I cared.

This respondent reports having been similarly cruel to a friend's pet dog when he was in grade school because the boy would often spend time with the dog rather the subject.

Another interviewee reports similar reasons for mistreating a roommate's cat: [I would] "just hurt enough to where it won't, to where it'll leave you alone. . . it won't jump on your clothes or get on the couch or get on the table." He continues:

---

9   My prompt.

If I didn't want it there that bad, it would be dead. I think the thing I really didn't like, what made me hate this cat, was my roommate went on an internship this semester and he didn't ask us if we'd take care of this cat. I mean he just like assumed that we would take care of it—feed it, clean out its litter box. He didn't even ask.

This respondent is evidently transferring his animosity toward his roommate to the roommate's cat.

In the case of both scapegoating an animal or exacting punishment upon them, the animals affected in these sorts of incidents are typically household animals that are familiar to the abuser. Though these abusers may feel somewhat regretful about their abusive acts and even have developed a general ethos that mistreating animals is not acceptable, they can ultimately quite readily justify such mistreatment to themselves.

Some of the interview data illustrates aggression being explicitly directed towards an animal, in this case a pet which had annoyed the interviewee:

My dog chewed the door from the house to the garage off the hinges—literally—and I severely beat him for it. I punched him as hard as I could in the head— it probably hurt my hand as bad as him. I've also kicked him for disobeying and tearing up other household items. I felt very bad, remorseful, but he doesn't listen. I've tried several types of punishments, but nothing seems to work. Not even beating. So I have ceased to punish him in this fashion.

Another respondent expresses the same sentiment of justified punishment, even in the case that such punishment might be violent or aggressive:

> My friend's father beat their dog scvcrcly. The dog bit me on the leg, not very hard or deep, but his father still beat the dog. [How did you feel about this incident?]   Felt the dog should have been punished, but not that severely.

Evidenced in both of these accounts is an ethos of physical punishment.   These young people may be acting upon smaller creatures for which they are responsible for training or managing in ways similar to those employed by parents and others to train and manage them.

The abuser may feel "bad" about how they have acted toward the animal, but they also rationalize that "something" had to be done to control the animal properly. More often than not that something tends to be expressed in a physical manner.   Caring for animal companions (and possibly younger siblings or babysitting charges) thus arguably becomes an early practice ground for the "cycles of violence" (Athens 1989; Widom 1992), which underlie the "discipline" practices of our culture.   As Straus and others such as Greven (1991) suggest with their work, the level of violence used in child rearing need not be severe or "abusive" to have a significant impact upon the child and how he or she relates with other human, and arguably non-human (Flynn 1999), beings.

In a number of cases, respondents recounted how their parents had disciplined a household pet, often in the same way in which they had disciplined the respondent as well. These accounts were typified by a physically aggressive orientation. For instance:

> When our dog would pee in the house, my mom
> would yell at it and rub its face in it and smack it
> and stuff like that.

In a few cases, respondents witnessed a respected adult
doing something terribly cruel to an animal without even
appealing to the rationale of "discipline." For instance, one
female respondent, who reported having never herself
effected any violence toward an animal, recalled observing
her uncle placing a firecracker in a cat's anus during a
family Independence Day gathering: "My uncle put the
firecracker up the cats butt and it exploded and everyone
laughed. I didn't; I just walked away, disgusted. It was
awful."

Also interesting, as a counterbalance to the pervading
paradigm of children mimicking adult discipline tactics,
was the account relayed by one study participant, who
reported enduring extensive abuse at the hands of his
father. He and his siblings were regularly and severely
beaten, as were the household pets. The subject found,
however, that he empathized with the family dog much
more than he did himself or his siblings:

> He [the subject's father] would do the same stuff to
> the dog he did to us…you know, kick it and throw it
> against the wall and stuff. I mean I just remember
> because it was a Dalmation and it was tall but it was
> skinny, so I mean when he would do it, it would
> really hurt the dog, you know. He [the dog] would
> just come over to us kids, but you could see the dog
> was broken, with his ears down and his eyes and
> face and everything down and his tail between his
> legs and you know, just everything, the dog was just
> broken, you know.

In a way, this respondent seems to identify with the dog, perhaps projecting some of his own feeling to the dog. Speaking about another dog the family had had, who had also suffered at his father's hands but had one day finally run off, he remarks that he hopes, "he found a better life somewhere." In fact, this respondent seemed to feel frustrated with himself because he had not stood up to his father. He seemed to rationalize that, in some way, he deserved the abuse because he reasoned that he could fight back but had not done so. He applied the same harsh logic to his siblings but not the family pet:

> I felt a kinship with the dog, 'cause the dog was, you know, going through the same things, so. I just felt worse for the dog, 'cause, you know, I could handle it, but the dog would like go up to my dad and want to play with my dad and my dad would start kicking at him.

Regarding siblings' crying at the abusive hands of his father, however, he says, "It'd just kind of like think, whatever, it happened. I'm surviving it. If it happens to you, you survive it."

Of the various factors which might characterize animal abuse, sex differences emerge as the most profoundly influential, with regard to their tendency to pattern the situation and style of abusive accounts reported. This next section considers some of the sex differences noted within this study's interview data.

Sex Difference in the Context of Reported Animal Abuse

Sex differences orient the most notable distinction with regard to the contexts under which animal abuse tends to occur. All but one of the interviewees who maintained throughout the interview that they had never abused an animal were women. Five of the six female interviewees who reported abuse described having engaged in abuse while at home, generally directing their actions toward household pets. A typical description of context for the females was:

> I had a friend over, and it was like, look at what the cat does when you put it under a blanket and you're hitting it!

There were several reports of placing animals in a blanket or sheet and swinging them around or otherwise teasing them. The same subject who recounts putting her cat in a blanket and hitting it also remarked that she and her sister were "generally nice to it (the cat). I mean we fed it, and bathed it, and well. . . " When I probed with the observation that cats generally do not like to be bathed, she noted that, indeed, the cat did not like to be bathed but that, "we'd intentionally put it in the bathtub, and it would hate being in the bathtub, and we'd wash it."

Another subject notes that she "got more angry than I've ever been at my first puppy." She recalls "yanking on her collar with the leash really hard and I almost basically dragged her because I was so angry." This study participant then notes that she kicked her dog once during that incident but never did so again because she felt so badly about hurting the dog.

Another woman reports being at a friend's house, where the household had pet rats and a pet cat. This respondent remarks that she and her friend would play the "popcorn game." When I asked her to describe the game, she said, "We took a blanket, and we put two rats in the blanket and we were like throwing it up in the air." She recalls that, one day, there were some guys present when they were playing the popcorn game with the rats. One of the guys put a cat in the blanket with the rats. The respondent notes that, "when we did it, it (the cat) hit the ceiling, and that was cruel." She recalls that the game stopped then, and the girl who resided at the house yelled at the respondent.

Men were much more likely to report abusing wild or stray animals in an outdoor setting, typically at a pond, while driving a car, or while at work. Of twelve male respondents, only one reported abusing a household pet or enacting abuse at home; three others reported "disciplining" a pet. Typical accounts from my male respondents are exemplified by the following excerpts:

- "You got to have an idea of how long it [a bottle rocket] is going to take before it blows up. Depending if you want it to blow up next to or not next to the animal. But a lot of the time the bottle rocket will just screech by and will scare them [the animal] to death anyway. Mostly it's just the reaction. Jumps in the air and hair all poofs out and takes out [sic] running."
- "We would if we caught an animal like a frog, um, it's likely that it would end up being run over by a bicycle. Like one of us would have a

bike and we, we'd run it over, um, so its guts would spill out."

- "We'd like try to shoot birds with BB guns and our mom wouldn't let us have any other guns besides that. But uh we'd just shoot random birds, sometimes woodpeckers. But we stopped doing that after a while."
- "Three of my friends and I had a BB gun and we started playing around with it. Shooting at a distance and then shooting smaller things and then moving things. And then we shot a squirrel on a tree."

These more characteristic male accounts offered by male respondents tend to feature fireworks and BB guns directed at birds and frogs or fish. Many times, the setting for these accounts is a small pond near a suburban setting. Most times, the motivation seems to be a variation on sensation-seeking i.e., "having something to do" so as to stave off boredom. Almost without exception, such acts occur in a small group of exclusively boys.

One man reported teasing pet cats while at home: "When my brother and I were little we used to mess with the cats a little, like when we were playing in the garage. We'd shut all the doors and chase them around. We never did anything to them, but they were scared running around." Except, however, for the three incidents in which male interviewees reported disciplining a household pet in what they ventured might have been an abusive manner, all other reports by men occurred outside their home environment.

The final consideration in this chapter summarizes portions of accounts wherein study participants talk about what, if anything, might have motivated them to stop abusing animals. Sometimes interviewees' accounts suggest they simply "outgrow" the behavior, but other accounts clarify a very memorable, traumatic event that motivated the interviewee to stop hurting animals.

Ending Abuse

I routinely noted, in analyzing these accounts, that quite a few of the individuals who had abused animals, usually in following along with a set of peers, would find themselves compelled to acknowledge the harm their behavior had caused. In some cases, this realization came in the midst of an act, perhaps because the animal bled or cried out in pain. Other times, an interviewee would express remorse upon coming to empathize with the animal in some other way. In some cases, of course, abusers simply seemed to outgrow their abusive behavior.

This experience of coming to identify with an animal one had abused is perhaps quite common. This sort of interaction was exemplified, for instance, in an episode of The Simpson's (Cohen 1998). Bart, under encouragement by the school bully, took aim at a nesting bird perched within a tree and hit it, killing the bird. Actually, Bart had tried to aim away from the bird, evidencing that he did not really want to shoot the bird at all but also did not want to look like a "wimp" in front of his peer. Once the bird was killed, however, Bart felt terrible. Noticing that the bird had been protecting hatchlings that were now motherless, Bart took it upon himself to take care of the baby birds.

Several particular accounts characterize the conditions under which an abuser might come to identify with the abused animal. In one case, this realization did not occur until quite awhile after the actual abuse had occurred. One woman spoke ruefully about the fate of the family cat she said she had abused and which, eventually, developed psychological problems and began urinating throughout the family's home. The respondent's mom did not realize what the respondent and her sister had been doing to the cat, and the mom eventually decided to send the cat to live with a family friend who had a farm. The respondent visited the cat some time later, noting that:

> She [the cat] was so skinny and little that, I mean she was so huge and just seemed more full of life than she did living on the farm and I felt guilty that I was the cause of her being, peeing all over the house, because I was mean, because I didn't— I mean I think about the blanket thing, where I hit her under the blanket a lot.. I didn't feel we were responsible enough, like, we maybe were the cause of why we got rid of her because she had a problem.

Usually, though, something during the abusive interaction prompts an abuser to feel pity for the animal. Consider the following observation:

> After we shot the bird, the other bird kept flying around the dying bird. Like it was grieving or something. It was weird to see a bird do that. I felt really bad about what I did.

In this case, a group of boys was shooting at birds with a BB gun. The respondent hit one of the birds and then remarked upon the surviving birds' reaction to its mate's (or perhaps its friend's) injury. The respondent had apparently not imagined that a bird might evince a human-like reaction such as grief.

For those who do not come to realize the harm they are causing, at least the idea seems to emerge that significant others— particularly, for straight males, female others— would disapprove of behavior such as abusing animals. This realization seems to occur as the young person finishes high school and moves on to college and more of an adult set of roles. Alternatively, in a few cases, there seems to emerge a gradual realization that animals might have feelings. For instance:

> There was a time when they [animals] were just there. They were living, but they didn't really have personalities. There was no humanity at all involved in it. Now, the boundaries have sort of shifted and I wouldn't [intentionally hurt an animal], just because it would be cruel.

More common, though, is the sentiment expressed by one study participant, articulating more of a self-interested stance, observing that, "girls wouldn't want to hang out with a guy that did that sort of stuff," in explaining why he curtailed his involvement in vandalism, shoplifting, and acts of animal cruelty. He had previously engaged in such behavior with his male peers. This reasoning process nicely illustrates Schur's (1973) observation in Radical Non-Intervention that, left along, many delinquent boys will correct their deviant behavior on their own, often in an effort to better impress female counterparts sought as romantic partners.

The onset of an adult mentality will of course vary depending upon the individual. For instance, an individual who graduates from high school and then takes a job directly, remains in the same town, and socializes with the same peer group is not likely to experience a significant role change, and thus his or her sentiment, or affective, structures are likely to remain constant. Only when this individual marries, has children, or otherwise alters his or her fundamental role structure would such changes be expected to occur.

There are a number of factors that are associated with abuse. Additionally, there are patterns with regard to gender and gender-based social scripts that characterize differences in the abuse reported by men, as opposed to women. Finally, there are certain components that characterize abuse incidents that lead to an abuser ceasing to abuse. Under such conditions, an individual may be "going along with the crowd" and engaging in an abusive act but then feel some connection with the abused animal and conclude that such behavior is inappropriate. The next chapter offers a model which connects some of the motivational explanations offered by the interviewees in this study.

CHAPTER VII

The Findings and Limitations of this Study

Is animal cruelty associated with human-directed violence?

This project's findings render it difficult to conclude whether or not there exists an empirical association between animal cruelty and human-directed aggression. While the quantitative findings indicate that there is no clear and concise association between animal cruelty and human-directed violence and thus contradict some of the claims made by the animal rights community (Ascione et al. 1999, Lockwood and Ascione 1998), these findings do not evidence that there is **no** relationship between animal cruelty and human-directed violence; clearly there is. I must therefore reject my first hypothesis, which proposes that there exists no association between animal cruelty and human-directed aggression.

The one conclusion that is most evident is that any association that does exist between animal cruelty and human-directed violence is decidedly complicated and nuanced. I could find no evidence that animal cruelty perpetuated during childhood or adolescence is associated with violence during adulthood. Once other childhood/teenage anti-social behaviors are incorporated into the model, any effect animal cruelty has on adult fighting behavior dissipates. Still, animal cruelty during childhood/adolescence does correlate with other childhood/adolescent measures of anti-social behavior. Examining a correlation matrix of animal cruelty and each of the other twelve childhood/adolescent anti-social behaviors included in this study, one notes that animal cruelty correlates with just about every other behavior, violent and non-violent. A factor analysis of animal cruelty and these other anti-social behaviors suggests, however, that animal cruelty associates most closely with the measures of violent childhood or teenage behaviors, such as fighting, hurting siblings, and bullying. Once this group of factors is regressed against adult violence, however, animal cruelty again fails to predict adult violence.

One dimension that might complicate the findings observed herein is that the measure of violence during adulthood used in this study is limited by the definitions of adult violence that are available within this data. I use the proxy measures of fighting and fighting with weapons to represent "adult violence." Note that I did have other measures such as child abuse and domestic violence, but, because the mean age of my sample was so low, these other measures did not prove very robust, even if considered as an index. Perhaps interviewing an older community sample would yield more insight into the correlation between animal cruelty and later violence throughout the life course.

While animal cruelty shows no predictive power in discerning who might go on to engage in fighting behavior as an adult, it may be a predictor for other types of violent adult behaviors that could not be represented in this study. For instance, animal cruelty may indeed discern between those who will go on to murder a human being and those who will not. To truly test this relationship empirically, however, one would need a study group comprising both murderers and non-murderers. If the entire such study group answered, for instance, a battery of DIS questions, logistic regression models could be created to examine empirically whether or not something like animal cruelty predicts whether or not one might engage in murderous behavior. As it stands, the "evidence" which links animal cruelty with such human-directed violence as murder or multiple murder relies only on data collected from the murdering group. Without a control group, it is impossible to know which behaviors demonstrate statistical predictive power (Harris 1977).

It is possible that a larger sample, for which there was more variability in the extent of animal cruelty reported, might find that extensive involvement in animal cruelty as a child does predict fighting behavior (or other violent behavior) in adulthood. As Kazdin (1990) finds with regard to firesetting, the frequency, duration, and context of anti-social behavior likely matters more than whether or not it was simply enacted. The sample used in this study is limited in several other ways. First, it was a community sample drawn from newspaper advertisements. Thus, it is not a systematic, representative sample. Additionally, the sample was drawn from a predominantly white, college town. Thus, there is likely to have been an oversampling of younger, more-educated people and an undersampling of non-whites.

While the quantitative results do not firmly clarify whether or not animal cruelty is associated more with violent and non-violent behaviors during childhood/adolescence, the qualitative results suggest that animal cruelty does demonstrate at least some association with non-violent, anti-social behaviors during the childhood and teenage years. For instance, many interviewees report engaging in animal cruelty as a means of sensation-seeking in much the same way they might engage in vandalism, stealing, or fire setting. However, the qualitative data also indicate mixed results, in that sometimes animal cruelty is effected by young people based upon an aggressive motivation extending from frustration. The next section of this chapter explores a sociologically-based model of why young people engage in animal cruelty. The advantage of a phenomenologically[10]-driven sociological model is that it extends the analysis afforded by a symptomological, quantitative analysis of indicator-based data to one in which process, experience, and the complexity of human motivation can be better incorporated.

---

[10] By phenomenological, I refer to the approach that Katz (1988) introduced to the study of deviance/criminal behavior. This method demands careful examination of the situations in which deviance and crime occur. Katz contends that it is in *the doing* of crime (and the recounting thereof) that the motivations and experiences of participants can be best understood.

A Sociological Model of Childhood/Adolescence Animal Cruelty

With regard to the context of abuse, I seek here to model the conditions under which reported abuse tends to occur. The quantitative findings suggest that animal abuse proffered during childhood/adolescence is correlated, at least to some extent, with non-violent delinquent acts, such as stealing, vandalism, and fire setting. The interview data provides more clarification as to the conditions under which animal abuse occurs, suggesting that some animal abuse seems to be characterized by a sensation-seeking motive and quite a lot of it also seems to be characterized by violent or aggressive motivations. Motivational categories indicated in the data include an imitation of behavior learned from adults and peers, an effort to express frustration, an attempt to clarify one's personal and social identity commitments, and a desire to seek sensation.

Chart 6.1, below, offers a model illustrating how these motivations might both relate to animal cruelty and interrelate with one another. Based upon the accounts provided in the interviews collected during this study, the model depicted in Chart 6.1 illustrates four factors that might motivate animal cruelty. Additionally, the model illustrates proposed interactions between these four variables.

Sensation-seeking and identity explorations, for instance, may interact in that an individual might attempt to explore a potential social identity by doing something with a group of peers so as to have something "exciting" to do. While engaging in an act of cruelty with the ostensible motivation of having something exciting to do, someone may find that they are unwilling to commit personally to a particular social identity. For instance, if someone is trying to hang with the "tough" guys and accidentally kills an animal during such a sensation-seeking adventure, he or she may draw some conclusions with regard to his or her identity commitments.

Chart 6.1. *A Model of Relationships Between Motivations Provided by Abusers*

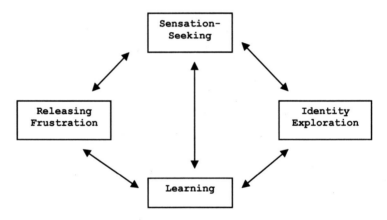

Similarly, identity exploration may interrelate with learning processes because one will inevitably be inclined to "try on" those identities with which one is familiar. In one's development, one is inclined to pursue identity options based upon imitation. For instance, if one's father is a hunter, one is more likely to try out hunting and to learn certain rules of hunting as they are embraced by one's father. One may try out hunting with one's father, however, and find that he or she is disgusted by it and thus unable to commit to this particular identity. Learning interacts with the release of frustrations in similar ways.

One is likely to imitate one's parent(s), older sibling(s), or peers when releasing frustration. One learns how to act after a bad day, for instance, by watching one's parent's behavior after returning from a difficult day at work. Alternatively, when one is feeling frustrated, one may also invent some release, which one may then internalize, or "learn," for future use.

The release of frustration very possibly interacts with sensation-seeking in that one might release aggression but then feel excited by its release. Alternatively, one may be doing something "for fun" but find that the activity serves to release a sense of frustration or aggression. Finally, sensation-seeking may in turn interact with learning processes. One may, for instance, learn to blow up frogs with firecrackers from a peer but then later find that one in fact enjoys doing this act.

The sections below explore in more detail some of the findings and conclusions generated by the interview data collected in the course of this study.

Identity Exploration

Individuals who demonstrate an inclination to most readily identify themselves as having abused animals seem either to be (a) highly remorseful about some incident of abuse, particularly if the incident resulted in the death or serious injury of the animal; or (b) inclined to have incorporated a "badass" identity (Katz 1988). Under the rubric of such an identity, engaging in mean, tough, or alien behaviors augments one's masculine worth (see also Athens 1989 and Gilligan 1997). What is intriguing is that several interviewees did not answer in the affirmative when asked DIS Question #9, yet during an in-depth interview detailed several cruel incidents to which they have been party. Effectively, they did engage in abuse, but they do not readily identify themselves as having been cruel to animals, i.e., they have not identified themselves with the role of "animal abuser." Identity-testing seems, then, to be one of the keys to understanding why young people abuse animals and how they experience such abuse.

I noticed that virtually none of my respondents fit the role of a truly committed "badass." Katz (1988) alludes, however, that there exist at least two variants of a "badass." Some "badass" characters are genuinely capable of being sadistic and malicious, but most may be seeking simply to project toughness and seem socially "alien" to mainstream adults and other "squares" so as to fit into a perceived "tough" social identity (Ulmer 2000). However, these individuals do not seem to instigate or particularly enjoy cruelty. Though several of my interviewees had been in trouble with authority figures and even in legal trouble, most did not evince a commitment to being truly mean or cruel.

What I observed in the accounts interviewees provided, however, was a recurring theme. Many interviewees had gone along with or even initiated abuse, but then something they did caused some harm to an animal, a harm to which the abuser could relate. For instance, an animal perhaps bled, died, or otherwise evinced a sense of suffering, and the abuser was emotively affected by this, activating a sense of guilt (Owens and Goodney 2000). Typically, after such an incident, an abuser will report that they avoided engaging in such abusive acts again, even amid peer pressure. Some admitted abusers, of course, never experienced such an incident and thus simply seemed to outgrow abusive behavior without incident, perhaps finding little social support for such acts as they took on more adult roles.

Broadly speaking, better understanding of the situational dynamics of violence is needed. What distinguishes an individual who instigates an incident of animal cruelty from someone who reports having simply gone along with a cruel act so as to fit in with a group of peers? How do people come to categorize those cruel acts in which they may have gleefully engaged from those that they felt "crossed the line"? A glimpse into the phenomenon of small-group violence as exemplified in these accounts of animal cruelty offers some insight into the phenomenological social dynamics of this violence. It is rare that such an event will be witnessed by a researcher or caught on videotape and thus we must rely on participants recounting their involvement in these activities.

Perhaps the process of abusing with a small group of friends has a normalizing influence upon some young people. Instigators of such acts are likely to have already normalized such "senseless" violence within their moral calculi. Effectively, they may be personally committed to a "badass" identity. This would be consistent with much of the deviance literature, specifically Sutherland's differential association (Sutherland and Cressey 1974) and Sykes and Matza's (1957) neutralization techniques.

Also relevant here is a consideration of the differences in social scripts that underlie variations in patterns of animal cruelty, particularly with regard to gender. Such social scripts extend from the availability of differing social roles according to one's gender. As Henry and Short (1954) observe, it is often easier for men to appropriate violent identities. Reifying this observation, Affect Control Theory (Heise 1979, as discussed in the first chapter) suggests that such normative role designations which categorize certain identities as masculine still apply fifty years later. Specifically, violent identities such as "thug," "murderer," or "robber" generate an image of a male in most Americans' minds.

Social scripts by which women might engage in abuse tend to be oriented to the home and family. As Schur (1984) notes, much of women's violence tends to occur in the home setting. Women are likely, when they do become violent, to enact violence towards a spouse or child. In fact, it may be that the reason we do not, as a society, consider women to be particularly violent is that the patterns of the violence they do engage do not tend to be officially counted. A woman must effectively kill a spouse before her violence towards him might be noted; though relatively few women kill a spouse or domestic partner, many more than might be expected report being violent or abusive toward a spouse or partner (Lottes and Weinberg 1997). Similarly, abuse of a child would need to be sufficient enough to warrant official intervention if it were to be noticed. Women who report having abused animals similarly note that their abuse tended to occur at home, often towards a household pet. Men were more likely to abuse an unknown (a stray or a neighbor's pet) or wild animal away from home.

Learning to Abuse

By the theory of differential association, or learning theory (Sutherland and Cressey 1974), some individuals may learn that aggression toward animals may be appropriate if one is trying to "teach" the animal to behave "properly." Several of the accounts listed in the qualitative results chapter above, recount an occasion during which an interviewee "disciplined" a pet, often in the same way that the interviewee him or herself had been disciplined and always in the way in which he or she had observed the pet being disciplined by a parent or other adult.

If a pet dog, for instance, urinates in the house, it is a good bet that a young person in that house will rub the animal's nose in the urine. The young person may also smack the pet, as they have seen a parent do. One can observe this same sort of behavior within sibling sets. An older child will inevitably attempt to "discipline" a younger sibling in the same ways in which an adult has disciplined him or her. The older sibling may correct their younger sibling in a tone that sounds very much like their adult role model's. The older sibling may even smack the younger sibling or take something away from the younger sibling by way of punishing the youngster.

The subject who reports having been extensively and brutally beat by his father has a story that echoes the ideas recounted in Athens' study of abused children— particularly boys—and the cycle of violence that may lead such children to themselves become violent. The first step of that cycle is to be victimized by violence as a child and, unable to defend one's self, to feel hapless and weak (Athens 1989). Such a child is typically inclined to view him or herself as worthless or weak-willed, hence the self-condemnation evidenced in the account reported in the previous chapter, which illustrates an interesting twist upon the cycles of abuse paradigm. In some cases, such as this, however, that cycle of abuse can be curtailed by an abused youngster realizing, in this case by empathizing with a beloved pet, that abuse is something he detests and will thus likelynever perpetrate on his own children.

According to the theory of differential association, people learn not only to act in the ways mentored by significant others, but they also learn how to rationalize, or explain, why and when it is acceptable to act in those ways. Thus one learns not only a repertoire of acts, but also the explanatory tracks that go with these acts by way of rendering them more socially acceptable. For instance, one perhaps learns that it is acceptable to hit the dog if it soils the carpet.

Not only will a young person learn behaviors and the associated moral reasoning from adults, but he or she will also learn from his or her peers to try certain acts. For instance, one might not reason, on one's own, that it might be "fun" to paint the dog, but one might get the idea from an older sibling. Similarly, one might get ideas of things to do to animals from television and movies. Again, an older sibling or peer may be the one to decide it would be "a good idea" or "a lot of fun" to try and re-enact a scene from a film with the family cat (e.g., do cats really land on their feet if dropped from the roof?), but the younger sibling might learn from this that it is appropriate or even especially "cool" to do such things.

As suggested earlier, there are arguably some interesting connections between learning and sensation-seeking, particularly among peers. One's friend or sibling might introduce the idea of abusing an animal, but after engaging in such behavior, some individuals will find that they enjoy the behavior, or even feel a release of frustration from it. Consider the interviewee who reports obvious enjoyment at "euthanizing" an animal. He had learned to abuse animals from an older sibling and peers, but through his own participation, he arguably incorporated a behavior he enjoyed and later came to use as a means of releasing tension. Now, as an adult, he seems to find some cathartic release from his occasional chance to "euthanize" an animal.

Releasing Frustration

Several accounts provided by interviewees did suggest that some of the study participants engage in animal cruelty as a means of releasing day-to-day frustrations. This is the most commonly-suggested explanation as to why people abuse animals that is given by animal rights groups and their researchers. By their reasoning, the idea that animals might be a "practice" realm for eventual violence against humans, termed the "graduation hypothesis," might make sense. However, examining the context under which even frustration-driven abuse is reported, such reasoning does not make as much sense.

Sometimes, this type of abuse is directed toward a pet belonging to a person with whom the abuser might be frustrated. This is the one frustration-driven scenario under which the graduation hypothesis might be plausible. Harming a person's pet because you are frustrated with them could graduate into hurting them directly. However, it may also indicate that the abuser views hurting another person as taboo. Thus, he or she may be able to rationalize harming another person's beloved pet, and may even feel a thrill in doing so, but will be unable to cross the line they have drawn against doing physical harm to another person. Individuals who do not draw such a distinction are likely to physically harm not just the animal but also the owner.

Another type of frustration-driven abuse occurs when a frustrated individual encounters an animal rather unexpectedly. On those occasions the individual may have been having a bad day, and might take advantage of the animal's availability or vulnerability. Under these circumstances, the abuser's frustration may be more generalized. The animal just happens to, effectively, be in the wrong place at the wrong time. Such individuals may be just generally frustrated with their life circumstances and feel sufficiently comfortable morally to take their frustration out on the animal.

Morally, these acts seem best facilitated when the individual can rationalize that the harm is serving some good, for instance that the animal is hurt and needs to be put out of its misery. Sometimes, accounts like this generate when the individual observes an animal being hit by a car or otherwise injured and then decides to "help" ease the animal's suffering by "putting it out of its misery." It is evident, though, that this "aid" feels very satisfying to the perpetrator. A similar sort of event occurs sometimes when someone is having a bad day and driving home from work. He or she may see an animal by the side of the road and swerve to hit it, often on a whim, so that he or she might release a bit of the generalized frustration he or she is feeling.

Finally, there are still other occasions wherein the animal itself is causing or, more likely, aggravating existing frustration, so that the individual may strike out at the animal to alleviate this tension. Here, the aggression shown toward the animal may not be anything the person would be willing to direct toward an adult peer. Rather, he or she may simply have integrated a rationale under which physical punishment of an annoying animal or child is appropriate. The section (above) exploring learning processes discusses this dynamic in more detail. Though this behavior may be learned, and thus easily rationalized, it will still often serve to release feelings of aggression. Here, again, the idea of a "graduation" hypothesis does not necessarily make sense. Rather, Arluke's reasoning (1999) seems a better explanation; in their study, animal abusers went back and forth between animals and humans. Some abused an animal and, later, a human, and then again an animal. Others abused a human first and then, later, an animal. Flynn's (1999) and, later, Curries (2006) research on animal cruelty as correlated with domestic violence suggests a similar, mixed pattern. In cases of domestic violence, abusers might abuse a spouse, kids, and family pets. In such cases, then, it would seem that there may be, for some people, certain categories of people and animals with whom it is acceptable to use physical aggression. Thus, while one might take out frustration in a physical way upon a household pet or a child, or even a spouse, he or she would not express aggression in a physical manner toward a co-worker, boss, teacher, or pastor.

Sensation-Seeking

The 21st century in America is increasingly dominated by a "mass society" culture, characterized by sprawling, un-centered cities which have emerged from the post-industrial redefinition of economically-desirable skills. While American society has always been characterized by small, isolated towns, the social structure afforded by a town square is now frequently usurped by the dominance of a Walmart or other major shopping chain, reachable only by car (Duany et al. 2001).

Bored young people seem to be left wondering what they might do "for some excitement" (Elias and Dunning 1986). Adolescence has long been an ambiguous stage of life with regard to role definitions and their associated activities. By its very modern structure, i.e., since the post-World War II era, adolescence serves as an extended "holding pen" designed to delay young people's entry into the workforce by as long as possible, presumably so that they can gain marketable skills (Felson 1998). In fact, though, schooling is increasingly generic and aimed to "process" ever-larger mega-schools rendering it not particularly challenging or engaging for most students. Additionally, work opportunities for teens are limited in the increasingly competitive American economy. Hence, young people are left bored and may look for mischief.

When men talk of their boyhood cruelty toward animals and other such anti-social engagements (shoplifting, vandalism, fire setting, etc.), they recount these stories using a vocabulary that highlights the concept of sensation-seeking (Matza 1964b). This rhetoric echoes Katz's (1988) exploration of thrill-seeking among shoplifters. Stories provided him by young people who had engaged in shop-lifting suggests that these youngsters did not shoplift because they particularly needed, or even wanted, the items they stole. The motivation for the behavior is explicitly and consistently articulated as being the feeling of excitement that is garnered by feeling as though one has gotten away with something.

Many accounts of animal abuse evince this same rubric of expression. Maybe reported abusers recount experiencing the abuse as something that was fun, or, often, funny. Most such accounts feature settings wherein abusers felt there was "nothing to do." Many times, the account features alcohol consumption and an impromptu opportunity to do something to an unsuspecting animal. The young people, for instance, may be sitting around on a porch, perhaps drinking, feeling bored. A neighborhood cat might happen by, and someone will suggest doing something to the cat, selling the idea as something potentially "hilarious." The others in the group may go along, excited to have something to do. As some accounts suggest, however, behavior that begins with the motivation of relieving boredom via seeking sensation can turn into an unexpectedly negative experience if the animal is killed or injured in such a way as to emotively affect the abuser.

Conclusion

Though each case of animal cruelty is unique, we can see some patterns in its motivations. Additionally, we can see crossovers in motivations in that some accounts incorporate multiple motivational forces. Moreover, it seems evident that such acts usually tell richer tales of social dynamics and dysfunctions than they do of any particular individual's pathologies.

CHAPTER VIII

Conclusions and Implications: How Understanding the Social Construction of Animal Cruelty Helps Clarify Other Acts of Juvenile Delinquency

Animal cruelty is but one of many kinds of behaviors that are commonly categorizes as juvenile delinquency. Animal cruelty, as has been explored herein, is, however, more likely to be considered a serious act than are other kinds of delinquency, such as shoplifting or lying. And, though most acts of animal cruelty are probably no more serious than shoplifting or vandalism in terms of the developmental psychology of the young perpetrator, some young people seem to be demonstrating a new kind of "extreme" violence: school shootings, "bumfights," "wilding," etc. Are these acts really more common and, if so, why? Or, do these acts simply generate moral panics played out on the always-hungry stages of talk-show TV and twenty-four hour news networks?

Gottfredson and Hirshi's (1990) identify ineffective parenting (defined as parents not recognizing and punishing deviant behavior) as the major "cause" of low self-control in future adults. A punitive approach to socialization, however, virtually ensures that a child will not develop his or her own "spirit of discipline" (Piaget 1997:361). Discipline in our society is largely meted out via punishment and negative reinforcement (i.e., "Don't do that!"). Explanation and reasoning are seldom given much attention, aside from in the idealized family dramas enacted on television, such as in the TV show *7th Heaven*. As Piaget (1997:363) argues, "it may very well be that it is in spite of adult authority that the best of our young people sooner or later adopt a disciplined way of living," or, as he argues, a compassionate outlook toward others.

Ironically, as we give less time and attention to our children as a social priority, overwrought parents are left with too little time and too many demands. The familial conditions inherent to this period in history— busy parents, broken families, overcrowded classrooms, "latchkey" kids, and a hegemonic mass media (Postman 1994)— arguably underscore the desire for a simplified means of identifying at-risk youth. Such approaches, however, tend toward demonizing young people and minimizing our cultural responsibility for their behavior. Thus, when "good," middle-class youth violently act out, "civilized" society is left grasping for explanations which incorporate biological or parental attributions rather than a social or collective sense of responsibility. Modern, round-the-clock, instant access media only helps to generate a "panic" mindset, leading many people to think there is some new and terrible outbreak in teen violence/deviance. In fact, concern over "out of control" teens has characterized American society for the past many decades (Cohen 1972; also, see Ron Mann's film *Grass* [1999] for an excellent depiction of historical panics over young people's marijuana use).

We want quick warning signs by which to identify the children who might be most likely to become problems. The difficulty is that these warning signs are typically constructed via reverse engineering. Children who turn into monsters are examined under a microscope. Anything "intuitively" evil is suspect. Past engagement in animal cruelty, for instance, might be identified as a culprit. Looking rigorously, however, we can see that many young people engage in animal abuse, often quite coldly and callously. Still, few of these young people go on to engage in adult human violence. It is our responsibility as researchers to guarantee that "helpful" indicators of assumed social problems have been carefully tested because they now have considerable policy import, as any young person who likes to wear black and play video games might report:

> I still feel kind of uncomfortable here; the kids have so much money. I think of myself as somebody different. And since the thing in Colorado, we get looks from everybody. After those shootings, they talked about the warning signals, and they're describing kids like us. What am I supposed to do with that? *(from a student at an Arizona high school, as reported by The New York Times* [Martin 1999]*).*

To make monsters of the modern alienated teen is to follow suit with prior eras, wherein marijuana, car racing, and rebellious hair or dance styles were demonized. To do so however, ensures us no better understanding than "the confused impressions of the crowd" (from Spaulding and

Simpson's translation of Durkheim's Suicide, 1951:41). Extending Durkheim's perspective and presuming that animal cruelty may indeed be an indication more of social than individual patterns, the moral consensus that animal cruelty is inhumane seems to be strongly counterbalanced by the reality that many of us have, at times, been cruel toward animals.

School Shooters

While the Columbine shootings represented the culmination of a year of violent school shootings during the 1998-99 school year, rendering that particular school year uniquely violent, school shootings in fact are not an historical anomaly. One of the more infamous cases dates back to 1979 and was perpetrated in San Diego by a young woman, 17-year-old Brenda Spencer. She shot up the elementary school across the street from her home with a gun she received for Christmas.

What was unique to the school shootings of 1998-99 was that there were so many of them in such quick succession. Newman (2004) in the book *Rampage* explore the phenomenon by visiting the town of each of that year's school shootings and doing in-depth interviews with members of each community. Their study documents a complex web of factors, conflating around the nexus of rural, insulated societies, isolation and boredom, and a desire for attention mixed with feelings of desolation on the part of the shooters.

In the case of Columbine, for instance, shooters Dylan Klebold and Eric Harris proved a deadly pair. Had Klebold never met Harris, he might not have ever done such a thing. However, Harris and Klebold proved a nasty match. For months, they had plotted a militaristic attack on their school, but Harris had applied to the Marines. He was turned down because he had taken anti-depressants, and in the same week was rejected by the college of his choice and his date to the prom. This series of rejections arguably pushed Harris over the edge. Had any of these factors gone differently, that terrible day might never have happened. Harris and Klebold might have joked years later about their "plots" against their high school.

The societal reaction that our teens are "out of control" that unfolded after Columbine did more, arguably, to underline the racial, ethnic, and socio-economic divisions within our society than it did to address the supposed danger within America's schools. In fact, still, the chance of any particular child being shot at school was low, but for mainstream, white, upper and middle class parents, seeing blonde, blue-eyed middle-American kids being shot to pieces in the schoolyard rattled them. In the 1980s, the gang violence that plagued youngsters in urban centers served only to keep white suburbanites locked up in their gated communities. In cities like Detroit and Philadelphia, white suburbanites abandoned the urban core. But, this did little to affect their everyday life. Seeing seemingly senseless violence seeping into their communities, however, beset these affluent white communities with a moral panic. Teens were out of control and needed to better monitored and managed. Still, most wealthy or upper-middle class teens who were identified for relatively petty crimes were excused just as many of the school shooters of the 1998-99 school year had been, but any teen who did anything truly violent was likely to face adult court and life sentences or even the death penalty. Meantime, teens from urban areas and working-class or rural communities were facing more hyper vigilant monitoring and punishment.

"Bum Fights"

One behavior that has been receiving increased media scrutiny, appearing recently on both the "Dr. Phil" show and *60 Minutes*, is "bum fighting." Young people are, in increasing numbers, reportedly beating up and even killing homeless people (Bradley 2006). It is theorized that teens are watching videos from a series called "Bum Fights" that is marketed by Indecline Films via the www.bumfights.com web site by a 23-year-old man named Ryan McPherson. McPherson promises people $100 to $1000 for clips they send in of "bum fights" they incite. Some teens seem to be mimicking the behavior they see on tape, either finding homeless people to beat up or inciting homeless people to fight one another and then videotaping these acts. Homeless people are characterized as "outsiders," or less than human. The videos portray the fights as comical, almost cartoon-like. That some young people might imitate such behavior is not implausible. In fact, such attacks seem to parallel "wilding" attacks by young people on unsuspecting strangers that were commonly reported a few years back and were also typically videotaped (as, by the way, are not a few acts of animal cruelty). Such incidents of small-group, all-male violence among adolescents also sounds eerily familiar to the rape and murder of Teena Brandon/Brandon Teena, a transgendered individual whose story is recounted in the film *Boys Don't Cry* (1999).

Arguably, this could be similar to the phenomenon of animal cruelty as it is detailed in the narratives presented in Chapter 5 of this text. Bored and seeking something "exciting" to do, young people—in particular small groups of males—go out seeking some excitement. They might see a hapless homeless person and decide to act out against him or her. It is my guess that, just as within many of the incidents of animal cruelty, one person probably starts the act and then cajoles the others to participate.

This phenomenon of small group violence can be seen in other situations, as well, such as the case of the 1998 dragging death of James Byrd in Jasper, Texas. There were three men that killed Mr. Byrd. One, John William King, 24, was clearly the ring-leader. Another had a developmental condition that rendered him much less mature than his chronological age; he simply seemed to go along with the leader. The third knew the group was doing wrong but was too intimidated to stand up to the leader and so he went along, doing as little as possible to actually participate. In an interview later, this man tried to claim that, though the leader was tattooed in racial epithets, this third man had never used the "N" word and did not believe in any of those idea. I find this hard to believe; this third man likely shared the racist attitudes of the leader. However, I do think that this third man was probably caught in the moment. He probably would not have done something like this on his own, much as Dylan Klebold probably would not have had he never met Eric Harris. When these behaviors occur, it is likely because there is one individual who likely comes from an at-risk or violent background who then influences others to "go along."

Finding the Dangerous Needles among the "Boys Being Boys"

Rather than attempting to effectively profile all teens, it would be more prudent to watch for those teens that come from troubled home environments. However, what this often means to people is homes where a child is very evidently being abused or neglected. Many times, an abusive home environment is one where the child is erratically punished, sometimes very harshly. It is a home where the child is derided and ridiculed and where he or she must watch a parent or siblings being similarly derided, ridiculed, or even beaten. These sorts of things, where there is aggressive, erratic parenting, happens in far too many American homes, but it is something that, in a culture that is quite accepting of the adage, "Spare the rod, spoil the child," gets overlooked. And so, these kids, who potentially might really be dangerous, who are learning to be violent by their caretakers and learning the neutralization techniques to justify this violence as well, are missed until, one day, they snap. Once they have snapped, we then parade them on CNN and TV shows like *American Justice* or Oxygen Network's new *Snapped*, which seems to profile violent teenage girls, warning that these were "normal" kids who just suddenly became violent one day. But, people do not just become violent one day. The young person, or the "mastermind" of such acts, if there is more than one youngster, has been, effectively, socialized for violence well before he or she "snapped." By demonizing all teens as potentially violent, we attempt to neutralize our own responsibility for condoning violent parenting and ignoring dangerous situations in seemingly "normal" homes.

Post-Columbine and especially now in the post 9/11 environment, at-risk teens have become even more scrutinized (FBI 2000). Previously dismissed pranks such as calling in a bomb threat during finals week are now being prosecuted under terrorism laws. Young, middle-class Americans are being labeled "terrorists" and given harsh sentences for such behavior. With TV shows warning of dangerous teens and teens gone wild, it is easy to rationalize that such harsh punishment is merited. Is it really though? Or are young people just being young people. The juvenile justice system was created because it was understood that young people do not possess the same decision-making capabilities of adults. And, though they may dress and act like twenty-something's, indeed, these children do not possess the logical and evaluative faculties that their twenty-something peers do.

Subjecting such young people to adult criminal court and even adult correctional facilities only ensures that these children are truly hardened. Could we, as Schur (1973) suggests, find a way to overlook much of this behavior and allow children to simply grow out of such phases? Of course, a child who murders might not be able to be overlooked so easily, however, even in this case, would it not seem plausible that such a child could be reformed?

In effect, if such labels such as "thug" or "killer" tend to connotate images of men in most citizen's minds (per Affect Control Theory—see Heise 1979 and MacKinnon 1994), a young man who starts to traverse a deviant pathway might find that such labels are applied to him as in, "this is where you are headed." Courts and correctional systems may think that they are trying to curtail a problem before it becomes too severe. This embodies the "scared straight" approach. In effect, we seem to think that, if we come down hard and fast on a troubled child, they will get scared and choose a better course. Human behavior is not so simple, though. Young people often engage in, especially negative, behavior for irrational reasons. In the end, such a young man might instead tend to internalize such a label via the "looking-glass" self process (Cooley 1902). Thus, the label will carry more power over a longer period of time, thereby potentially proving more salient in terms of identity structure than it was ever intended to be.

The impetus to punish young people for what amounts to school pranks arguably extends from an overflow of funds being diverted to "protecting" schools from terrorist attacks. Schools apply for these funds and then have to justify their efforts. The teenage prankster becomes a natural target for such enforcement. In the same way, as the correctional system has expanded over the last twenty-five years, the juvenile part of this system has followed the overarching paradigm. In effect, there is a financial need for "dangerous" teens to now fill these facilities and employ the workers within them. The more dangerous teen who, for instance, have murdered another person are typically transferred to adult facilities. So, who is left behind to fill the beds?

How might we better socialize young people to be empathetic?

Bandura (1990:43) suggests that: "civilized conduct requires social systems that uphold compassionate behavior and renounce cruelty." Outwardly, our society does just that. However, our culture also clearly accommodates all sorts of cruel images and ideals. The discipline norms embraced by the vast majority of parents are replete with violence (Greven 1991; Strauss 1994). Our television and film media display scores of violent images during almost any given hour of programming. More than simply the wide availability of such images however, is the way in which certain identities are portrayed. Officially, "Officer Friendly" is the way in which middle-class children are taught to think of a police officer. But this ideal is hardly confirmed by the "real cop" shows that many of these young people watch quite regularly. Children are taught to be honest and noble, but can the movies they love depict more ambiguous characters, such as Dirty Harry, garnering the most social respect.

Piaget (1997), extending Durkheim's (1964) consideration of modern, industrial society, argues that children effectively manage two moral codes. The first is a solidarity-styled system marked by constraint and hierarchy. Familiar adults such as parents or teachers, as well as older peers, are largely simply obeyed based upon their social authority. As the child matures, however, he or she ideally acquires a "common morality" (Piaget 1997:351), which is inferred based upon a reasoned integration of the moral codes that govern the various social relations that the child maintains. As the child becomes capable of taking the role of the other, i.e., as s/he incorporates Mead's (1934) concept of a "generalized other", he or she becomes more inclined toward a cooperative morality. This, argues Durkheim (1964), is the sort of moral code we would expect to emerge in an advanced, differentiated society. As people become more individuated, they are expected to take more responsibility for themselves and to govern themselves via an internalized "spirit of discipline" (Piaget 1997:361).

Unfortunately, if we consider Postman's reasoning in *The Disappearance of Childhood*, we must question how effectively a common morality is being internalized in a society that is increasingly dominated by mass media. As Green et al. (2004) suggest, in a discussion of why many people so deeply enjoy watching television and movies, that TV allows viewers to effectively transport into a narrative world but that such narrative cannot be considered interaction *per se*, since social interaction necessitates that we encounter forceful, demanding, real others. Real interaction forces us to stand before Cooley's (1902) looking-glass and adjust our presentation of self to ensure more pleasant cooperation with others. Television, while it can provide "company" and simulate "interaction," is not at all similar to real interaction that necessitates constantly taking on the role of the other so as to consider how to keep the other person content and engaged.

In effect, by not interacting with real others and thereby being forced to negotiate and incorporate their needs and demands, one potentially becomes anti-social and impatient, perhaps preferring the "simplicity" of televised "companions" and virtual relationships. How can we expect young people in this society to act in compassionate ways when we too often raise them within a home environment in which violence is tolerated as a means of enacting power and discipline and then, increasingly, do not—as a society—facilitate the sort of interaction which would allow them to learn empathy and self-discipline? That animal cruelty is in fact quite common and not especially correlated with human-directed violence should perhaps frighten us, as a society, more than if it were unusual and reliably predicted individual social-psychological pathology.

APPENDIX A

Diagnostic Interview Schedule (DIS) Items

DIS BEHAVIOR CHECKLIST

Subject #_____

Date Administered _____ __ _______

Administered By _____

1. When you were a child or a teenager, did you frequently break the rules at home or at school?	No___ Yes___
2. When you were a child or a teenager, did you frequently get into trouble with the teacher or principal for misbehaving in school?	No___ Yes___
3. When you were younger, were you ever blamed for cheating in schoolwork or in games with your friends?	No___ Yes___
4. Were you ever suspended from school?	No___ Yes___ If Yes – How many times? ____
5. Were you ever expelled from school?	No___ Yes___ If Yes – How many times? ____
6. Did you ever play hooky from school?	No___ Occasionally___ Frequently___

7. Did you ever get in trouble with the police, your parents or neighbors because of fighting (other than with siblings) outside of school?)	No___ Occasionally___ Frequently___
8. Did you ever use a weapon (like a stick, gun or knife) in a fight?	No___ Occasionally___ Frequently___
9. When you were a child or a teenager, were you ever mean or cruel to animals, or did you intentionally hurt animals (mammals, not insects, etc.)?	No___ Occasionally___ Frequently___
10. When you were young, did people ever complain that you bullied or were mean to other children?	No___ Occasionally___ Frequently___
11. When you were a child or a teenager, did you ever intentionally hurt you siblings or other children seriously enough to cause notice by parents/surrogates?	No___ Occasionally___ Frequently___
12. When you were a child or a teenager, did you ever run away from home overnight?	No___ Yes___
13. Of course no one tell the truth all the time, but did you tell a lot of lies when you were a child or a teenager?	No___ Yes___
14. Have you ever used a false name or an alias?	No___ Yes___

15. When you were a child, did you more than once swipe things from stores or other children, or steal from parents or from anyone else?	No___ Yes___
16. Have you ever taken money or property from someone else by threatening to use force, like snatching a purse or robbing them?	No___ Yes___
17. When you were a kid, did you ever intentionally (on purpose?) damage someone's car or house or do anything else to destroy someone else's' property?	No___ Yes___
18. When you were a child or a teenager, did you ever set any fires you were not supposed to?	No___ Yes___
19. Were you ever arrested as a juvenile or sent to juvenile court?	No___ Occasionally___ Frequently___
20. Have you ever been arrested since you were 18 years old for anything other than traffic violations?	No___ Occasionally___ Frequently___
21. Have you had at least 4 traffic tickets in your life for things like speeding, running a red light or causing an accident?	No___ Yes___

22. Have you forced someone else to have sex when they didn't want to using physical force or threat of physical force?	No___ Yes___
23. Have you ever had an affair with a married person?	No___ Yes___
24. During (any) marriage, did you have sexual relations outside of marriage with at least 3 different people (heterosexual or homosexual)?	No___ Occasionally___ Frequently___
25. Have you ever been paid money to have sex with someone?	No___ Yes___
26. Have you ever had sex with someone in order to obtain drugs?	No___ Yes___
27. Have you ever made money by finding customers for prostitutes or call girls or male prostitutes?	No___ Yes___
28. Have you ever made money outside the law by buying or selling stolen property or selling drugs or running numbers?	No___ Yes___
29. Have you ever done anything that you could have been arrested for if you had been caught?	No___ Yes___
30. Have you ever gotten into trouble because you had spent too much money?	No___ Yes___

31. As an adult, have you failed to pay debts that you owed or failed to take care of other financial responsibilities that people expected you to take care of (examples: child support, loans)?	No___ Yes___
32. Have you ever intentionally written a bad check?	No___ Yes___
33. Have you ever been sued for a bad debt or had things you bought taken back because you didn't meet payments?	No___ Yes___
34. Did you ever walk out on your husband or wife (partner with whom you were living with as if married) either permanently or at least a few weeks?	No___ Yes___
35. Did you ever hit or throw things at your husband or wife (partner you were living with as though you were married)?	No___ Yes___
36. Have you ever spanked or hit a child (yours or anyone else's) hard enough that he or she had bruises or had to stay in bed or see a doctor?	No___ Yes___
37. Have you ever been accused of child abuse, or been the subject of a complaint on a child abuse hotline?	No___ Yes___

38. Since age 15, have you been in more than one fight that came to swapping blows other than fights with your husband or wife (partner you were living with as though you were married)?	No___ Yes___
39. Since you were 15, have you ever used a weapon like a stick, knife, or gun, in a fight?	No___ Yes___
40. Since you were 15, have you ever physically attacked anyone (other than while fighting)?	No___ Yes___
41. Since you were 18, did you ever hold three or more different jobs within a five year period?	No___ Yes___
42. Have you been fired from more than one job?	No___ Yes___
43. Since you were 18, have you ever quit a job three times or more before you already had another job lined up?	No___ Yes___
44. Have you ever thought you lied pretty often since you have been an adult?	No___ Yes___
45. Have you ever traveled around for a month or more without having any arrangements ahead of time and not knowing how long you were going to stay or where you were going to work?	No___ Yes___

46. Has there ever been a period when you had no regular place to live, for at least a month or so?	No___ Yes___
47. Has there ever been a period when you did not provide the financial support to you children that you were supposed to?	No___ Yes___
48. Have you sometimes left young children under 6 years old at home alone while you were out shopping or doing anything else?	No___ Yes___
49. Have there been times when a neighbor fed a child (of yours/you were caring for) because you didn't get around to shopping for food or cooking, or kept your child overnight because no one was taking care of him or her at home?	No___ Yes___
50. Has a nurse or social worker or teacher ever said that any child of yours wasn't being given enough to eat or wasn't kept clean enough or wasn't getting medical care when it was needed?	No___ Yes___
51. Have you more than once run out of money for food for your family because you had spent the money on yourself or on going out?	No___ Yes___

52. Have you often felt that co-workers, neighbors or others were hostile towards you?	No___ Yes___
53. Have people often said that you did things deliberately to annoy or bother them (examples: arguing, teasing, or practical jokes until the other person gets angry)?	No___ Yes___
54. Have you sometimes enjoyed being mean (i.e., annoying badgering, harassing, hassling, etc.) toward other people)?	No___ Yes___
55. Have any of your friends or other people complained or gotten mad at you because you borrowed some of their things without their permission?	No___ Yes___
56. As an adult, do you change "best friends" frequently?	No___ Yes___
57. Have you often felt that people in authority (police, your boss, etc.) have gone out of their way to be difficult toward you, or to give you a hard time?	No___ Yes___
58. Was there ever a time when you really enjoyed outsmarting people in authority (like parents, your boss, or the police), to the point that you would often go out of your way to put something over on them?	No___ Yes___

59. As a teenager, did you ever intentionally spread rumors about someone (using letters, telephone calls or just talking with others) to hurt them, get back at them, or so that you could get something you wanted?	No___ Yes___
60. As a child or teenager, did you sneak out of the house at night when you were not allowed to, so that you could have some fun with friends?	No___ Occasionally___ Frequently___
61. Have you ever had the habit of exaggerating the truth about yourself, or lying about things you have done or experienced, to make yourself look good or better than others?	No___ Yes___

References

Abbott, Andrew, (1988). *The System of Professions: An Essay on the Division of Expert Labor*. Chicago: U-Chicago Press.

Anderson, Elijah (1999). *The Code of the Street: Decency, Violence, And the Moral Life Of The Inner City*. New York: W.W. Norton.

Arluke, Arnold (2002). "Animal Abuse as Dirty Play." *Symbolic Interaction* 25(4):405-431.

_____, J. Levin, C. Luke, and F. Ascione (1999). "The Relationship Between Animal Cruelty to Violence and Other Forms of Antisocial Behavior." *Journal of Interpersonal Violence* 14:245-253.

_____ and Randall Lockwood (1999). "Understanding Cruelty to Animals." *Society and Animals* 5:183-193.

Ascione, F. and Arkow, Eds. (1999). *Child Abuse, Domestic Violence, and Animal Abuse: Linking the Circles of Compassion for Prevention and Intervention*. West Lafayette, Indiana: Purdue University Press.

_____, C. Weber, and D. Wood (1997). "The Abuse of Animals and Domestic Violence: A National Survey of Shelters for Women Who Are Battered." *Society and Animals* 5:205-218.

_____ (1993). "Children Who Are Cruel to Animals: A Review of the Research and Implications for

Developmental Psychopathology." *Anthrozoos* 6:226-247.

Athens, Lonnie (1989). *The Creation of Dangerous, Violent Criminals*. New York: Routledge.

Bandura, A. (1990). "Selective Activation and Disengagement of Moral Control." *Journal of Social Issues* 46:27-46.

Becker, Howard (1990). "Generalizing from Case Studies." *Qualitative Inquiry in Education: The Continuing Debate.* Eds. E. W. Eisner & A. Peshkin, pp. 233-242. New York: Teachers College Press.

_____ (1963). *Outsiders: Studies in the Sociology of Deviance*. New York: The Free Press.

Becker, Kimberly, Jeffrey Stuewig, Veronica Herrera, and Lara McCloskey (2004). "A Study of Firesetting and Animal Cruelty in Children: Family Influences and Adolescent Outcomes." In *Journal of the American Academy of Child & Adolescent Psychiatry*. 43(7):905-912.

Block, Richard (1977). *Violent Crime: Environment, Interaction, and Death*. Lexington Press.

Boys Don't Cry (1999). Fox Searchlight Pictures.

Bradley, Ed (2006). "Bum Hunting." *60 Minutes*. October 1.

Chambliss, William, (1973). "The Saints and the Roughnecks" in *Society* 11(1):24-31.

Chesney-Lind, Meda (1998). *Girls, Delinquency, and Juvenile Justice*. Belmont, CA: Wadsworth

_____ (1997). *The Female Offender: Girls, Women, and Crime*. Thousand Oaks, CA: Sage.

Cohen, David S. (1998). *The Simpson's* Episode #5F22, "Bart the Mother." Original Airdate: September 27, 1998, on FOX.

Cohen, Stanley (1972). *Folk Devils and Moral Panics*. London: MacGibbon and Kee.

Cooley, Charles H. (1902). *Human Nature and the Social Order*. New York: C. Scribner's and Sons.

Currie, C. L. (2006). "Animal Cruelty by Children

Exposed to Domestic Violence." *Child Abuse and Neglect.* Apr (30)4:425-35.

Dahmer, Lionel (1994). *A Father's Story.* New York: William Morrow & Co.

Diagnostic and Statistical Manual of Mental Disorders IV (1994). Washington, D.C.: American Psychiatric Association.

Duany, Andres, E. Plater-Zyberk, and Jeff Speck (2001). *Suburban Nation: The Rise of Sprawl and the Decline of the American Dream.* New York: North Point Press.

Durkheim, E. (1951). *Suicide.* Translated by Spaulding and Simpson. Glencoe, IL: Free Press.

_____ (1964). *The Division of Labor.* New York: The Free Press.

Elias, N. and E. Dunning (1986). *Quest for Excitement.* Oxford: Blackwell.

Federal Bureau of Investigation (2000). *The School Shooter: A Threat Assessment Perspective.* Critical Incident Response Group. Quantico, VA: National Center for the Analysis of Violent Crime.

Felson, Marcus 1998. *Crime and Everyday Life, Second Edition.* Thousand Oaks, California: Pine Forge Press.

Felthous, A. R. and S. R. Kellert (1987). "Childhood Cruelty to Animals and Later Aggression Against People: A Review." *American Journal of Psychiatry* 144:710-17.

Fine, Gary Alan, (1986). "The Dirty Play of Little Boys." *Society* 24:63-67.

Flynn, J. (1999). "Animal Abuse in Childhood and Later Support Interpersonal Violence in Families." *Society and Animals* 7:161-172.

_____ (1988). "Torturing of Pets Could Be Prelude to Human Murderer." *San Francisco Examiner*, October 27.

Foucault, Michel (1975). *I, Pierre Riviere, Having Slaughtered My Mother, My Sister, and My Brother ...: A Case of Parricide in the Nineteenth Century.* Harmondworth: Penguin.

Franklin, Adrian (1999). *Animals & Modern Culture: A Sociology of Human-Animal Relations in Modernity.* Thousand Oaks, CA: Sage.

Gegax, T. Trend; Jerry Adler, and Daniel Pedersen. "The Boys Behind the Ambush." *Newsweek* (6 April 1998): 21-24.

Gilligan, James (1997). *Violence: Reflections on a National Epidemic.* New York: Vintage Books.

Glueck, Sheldon and Eleanor T. Glueck (1950). *Unravelling Juvenile Delinquency.* New York: Commonwealth Fund.

Goldstein, M. (1974). "Brain research and violent behavior." *Archives of Neurology.* 30:1-35.

Gottfredson, M. R. and T. Hirschi (1990). *A General Theory of Crime.* Stanford: Stanford University Press.

Green, Melanie C., Timothy C. Brock, and Geoff F. Kaufman (2004). "Understanding Media Enjoyment: The Role of Transportation Into Narrative Worlds." *Communication Theory.* 14(4):311-25.

Greven, P. (1991). *Spare the Child: The Religious Roots of Physical Punishment and the Psychological Impact of Physical Abuse.* New York: Knopf.

Hare, R. D. (1993). *Without Conscience: The Disturbing World of Psychopaths Among Us.* New York: Pocket Books.

_____ (1991). *The Hare Psychopathy Checklist-Revised.* Toronto: Multi-Health Systems.

Harris, Anthony (1977). "Sex and Theories of Deviance: Toward a Functional Theory of Deviant Type-Scripts." *American Sociological Review.* 42(1):3-16.

Heise, D. R. (1979). *Understanding Events: Affect and Construction of Social Action.* Cambridge: New York.

Hellman, Daniel S. and Nathan Blackman (1966). "Enuresis, Firesetting and Cruelty to Animals: A Triad Predictive of Adult Crime." *American Journal of Psychiatry* 122:1421-35.

Henry, Andrew and James Short (1954). *Suicide and Homicide.* New York: Arno Press.

Hensley, Chris and Suzanne Tallichet (2005a). "Animal
Cruelty Motivations." *Journal of Interpersonal
Violence* 20(11):1429-1443.
_____ (2005b). "Learning to be Cruel? Exploring the
Onset and Frequency of Animal Cruelty."
*International Journal of Offender Therapy and
Comparative Criminology.* 49(1):37-47.
Hickey, E. (1991). *Serial Murders and Their Victims.*
Belmont, Ca: Wadsworth.
Hirschi, Travis (1969). *Causes of Delinquency.* Berkeley:
University of California Press.
Hughes, S. (1998). *Breeds Apart: An Introduction to
Murder.* New York: CBS Worldwise, Inc.
Justice, Blair, Rita Justice, and Irvin Kraft (1974). "Early
Warning Signs of Violence: Is a Triad Enough?"
American Journal of Psychiatry 131:457-59.
Katz, Jack (1988). *Seduction of Crime: Moral and Sensual
Attractions in Doing Evil.* New York: Basic Books.
Kazdin, A. E., (1990). "Childhood depression." *Journal of
Child Psychology and Psychiatry.* 31(1):121-160.
Kellert, Stephen R. and Alan R. Felthous (1985).
"Childhood Cruelty toward Animals among Criminals
and Noncriminals." *Human Relations* 38:1113-29.
Kim, Jae-On and Charles W. Mueller (1977). "Introduction
to Factor Analysis: What It Is and How To Do It."
Quantitative Applications in the Social Sciences.
Thousand Oaks, CA: Sage Publications.
Kolko, D. J. and A. E. Kazdin (1989). "The Children's
Firesetting Interview with Psychiatrically Referred and
Nonreferred Children." *Journal of Abnormal Child
Psychology* 17:609-24.
Lemert, Edwin (1951). "Primary and Secondary
Deviation." *Social Pathology: A Systematic Approach
to the Theory of Sociopathic Behavior.* Pp. 75-78.
Liebman, F. (1989). "Serial Murders: Four Case Histories."
Federal Probation 53:41-45.
Locke, John (1705). "Some Thoughts Concerning
Education," in *The Works of John Locke in Nine*

Volumes, 12ᵗʰ Edition. 8:112-14. London: C & J Rivington.

Lockwood, R. and F. Ascione, Eds. (1998). *Cruelty to Animals and Interpersonal Violence: Readings in Research and Applications.* West Lafayette, IN: Purdue University Press.

Lottes, Ilsa and Martin Weinberg, 1997. "Sexual Coercion Among University Students: A Comparison of the United States and Sweden." *Journal of Sex Research* 34(1):67-76.

MacDonald, J. (1963). "The Threat to Kill." *American Journal of Psychiatry* 120:125-130.

MacKinnon, N. J. (1994). *Symbolic Interactionism as Affect Control.* Albany: State University of New York Press.

Mann, Ron (1999). *Grass.* Documentary produced by Home Vision Entertainment.

Martin, D. (1999). "Caution: Exploding Donkey." *The New York Times*, p. 3 of "Week in Review."

Masters, Brian (1993). *The Shrine of Jeffrey Dahmer.* New York: Coronet.

_____ (1985). *Killing for Company: The Case of Dennis Nilsen.* London: J. Cape.

Matza, David (1964a). *Delinquency and Drift.* New York: John Wiley and Sons, Inc.

_____ (1964b). *Becoming Deviant.* New Jersey: Prentice-Hall, Inc.

Mead, G. H. (1934). *Mind, Self, and Society from the Standpoint of a Social Behaviorist.* Chicago: University of Chicago Press.

Messerschmidt, James W. (1997). *Crimes as Structured Action: Gender, Race, Class, and Crime in the Making.* Thousand Oaks, CA: Sage.

Miles, Matthew B. and A. Michael Huberman (1994). *Qualitative Data Analysis: An Expanded Sourcebook,* 2ⁿᵈ Edition. Thousand Oaks, CA: Sage.

Muscari, Mary (2003). "Should I Assess for Animal Cruelty as Part of All Routine Child Health Visits?"

In *Medscape Nurses* (5):1.

Newman, J.P. (1987). "Reaction to Punishment in Extraverts and Psychopaths: Implications for the Impulsive Behavior of Disinhibited Individuals." *Journal of Research in Personality* 21:464-480.

Newman, Katherine S. (2004). *Rampage: The Social Roots of School Shootings*. New York: Basic Books.

Newton, Michael (1993). *Bad Girls Do It!: An Encyclopedia of Female Murders*. Port Townsend, WA: Loompanics.

Norris, J. (1988). *Serial Killers*. New York: Anchor Books.

Offord, D. R., M.H. Boyle, and Y. A. Racine (1991). "The Epidemiology of Antisocial Behavior in Childhood and Adolescence. In *The Development and Treatment of Childhood Aggression*, edited by D. J. Pepler and K. H. Rubin. Hillsdale, NJ: Lawrence Erlbaum Associates. Pp. 31-54.

Owens, Timothy and Suzanne Goodney (2000). "Self, Identity, and Moral Emotions across the Life Course." *Advances in Life Course Research, Volume 5: Self and Identity through the Life Course in Cross-Cultural Perspective*. 5:33-53.

Pearson, Patricia (1998). *When She Was Bad: How and Why Women Get Away With Murder*. New York: Penguin.

Piaget, J. (1997). *The Moral Judgment of the Child*. New York: Free Press Paperbacks.

Piper, Heather (2003). "The Linkage of Animal Abuse with Interpersonal Violence: A Sheep in Wolves' Clothing?" *Journal of Social Work*. Vol. 3, No. 2, 161-177.

Postman, N. (1994). *The Disappearance of Childhood*. New York: Vintage Books.

Price, J. M. and K. A. Dodge (1989). "Peers' Contribution to Children's Social Management." In *Peer Relationships in Child Development*, eds. T. J. Berndt and G. W. Ladd, pp. 341-70. New York: Wiley.

Pryor, Douglas W. (1996). *Unspeakable Acts: Why Men Sexually Abuse Children*. New York: New York University Press.

Rachels, James (2003). "Lectures on Ethics" by Immanuel Kant. *The Right Thing to Do*. New York: McGraw-Hill.

Raupp, C, M. Barlow, and J. Oliver (1997). "Perceptions of Family Violence: Are Companion Animals in the Picture?" *Society and Animals* 5:219-237.

Ressler, R., A Burgess, C. Hartman, J. Douglas, and A. McCormack (1986). "Murders Who Rape and Mutilate." *Journal of Interpersonal Violence* 1:273-87.

Rigdon, J. and F. Tapia (1977). "Children Who Are Cruel to Animals Follow-Up Study." *Journal of Operational Psychiatry* 8:27-36.

Robins, L. (1966). *Deviant Children Grown Up: A Sociological and Psychiatric Study of Sociopathic Personality*. Baltimore: The Williams and Wilkens Company.

Rubington and Weinberg (2005). *Deviance: The Interactionist Perpective (9ᵗʰ Edition)*. New York: Allyn and Bacon.

Sampson, Robert J. and John H. Laub (1995). *Crime in the Making: Pathways and Turning Points Through Life*. Cambridge, MA: Harvard University Press.

Schur, Edwin M. (1984). *Labeling Women Deviant: Gender, Stigma, and Social Control*. New York: Random House.

_____ (1973). *Radical Non-Intervention: Rethinking the Delinquency Problem*. Englewood Cliffs, NJ: Prentice-Hall.

Scully, D. and J. Marolla (1984). "Convicted Rapists' Vocabulary of Motives, Excuses, and Justifications." *Social Problems* 31:530-544.

Singer, Stephen and Chris Hensley (2004). "Applying Social Learning Theory to Childhood and Adolescent Firesetting: Can it Lead to Serial Murder? *International Journal of Offender Therapy and*

Comparative Criminology. 48(4): 461-76.

Strauss, M. A. (1994). *Beating the Devil out of Them: Corporal Punishment in American Families.* New York: Lexington Books.

Stryker, Sheldon (1968). "Identity Salience and Role Performance." *Journal of Marriage of the Family* 30:558-564.

Sullivan, Randall. "A Boy's Life: Kip Kinkel and the Springfield, Oregon Shooting (Part I)." *Rolling Stone Magazine* (17 September 1998):79-85.

Sutherland, Edwin H. (1937). *The Professional Thief: By a Professional Thief.* Chicago: University of Chicago Press.

Sutherland, Edwin and Donald Cressey (1974). "Differential Association." *Criminology* (pp.71-91). New York: J.B. Lippincott Co. (8th edition).

Sykes, G. M. and D. Matza (1957). "Techniques of Neutralization: A Theory of Delinquency." *American Sociological Review* 22:664-70.

Tallichet, Suzanne and Chris Hensley (2005). "Rural and Urban Differences in the Commission of Animal Cruelty." *International Journal of Offender Therapy and Comparative Criminology.* 49(6):711-726.

Tapia, F. (1971). "Children Who Are Cruel to Animals." *Child Psychiatry and Human Development* 2: 70-77.

Ulmer, Jeffery T. (2000). "Commitment, Deviance, and Social Control." *The Sociological Quarterly* 41(3):315-336.

Wax, D. E. and V. G. Haddox (1973). "Sexual Aberrance in Male Adolescents Manifesting a Behavioral Triad Considered Predictive of Extreme Violence: Some Clinical Observations." *Journal of Forensic Sciences* 19(1):102-8.

Weinberg, Martin S., and Colin J. William, and Douglas W. Pryor (1994). *Dual Attraction: Understanding Bisexuality.* New York: Oxford University Press.

Widom, C. (1992). *The Cycle of Violence.* Washington, D.C.: U.S. Dept. of Justice, Office of Justice Programs,

National Institute of Justice.
_____ (1986). *Sex Roles and Psychopathology.* New York: Plenum Press.
Zahn-Waxler, C., B. Hollenbeck, and M. R. Radka-Yarrow (1984). "The Origins of Empathy and Altruism." In *Advances in Animal Welfare*, ed. M. W. Fox and L. D. Mickley, pp. 21-41. Norwell, MA: Kluwar Academic.
Zaplin, Ruth T. (1998). *Critical Perspectives and Effective Interventions.* Gaithersburg, MD: Aspen Publishers.

Index

A

accounts, 3, 4, 12, 19, 28, 33, 37, 40, 41, 46, 58, 97, 100, 106, 107, 109, 111, 112, 113, 121, 124, 125, 127, 129, 130, 133, 134
advocate, 8, 9
Affect Control Theory, 36, 126, 143
anti-social, 4, 11, 12, 13, 21, 24, 25, 40, 42, 46, 47, 48, 50, 58, 63, 64, 66, 67, 70, 71, 74, 75, 76, 77, 78, 79, 81, 83, 85, 88, 89, 90, 91, 118, 119, 120, 133, 146
antisocial personality disorder, 5, 95

Arluke, 2, 3, 9, 12, 13, 15, 17, 18, 28, 41, 45, 96, 131, 157
Ascione, 3, 8, 15, 16, 18, 30, 33, 52, 117, 157, 158, 165
ASPCA, 8

B

bottle rocket, 98, 111
"bum fights," 140
butchers, 2, 3

C

cat, 98, 99, 100, 105, 107, 109, 110, 113, 128, 133
Chicago School, 29
Columbine, 138, 139
conduct disorder, 10, 50, 95